Mindset Before Matter Vol. 2

HOW TO BE A STARSHIP COMMANDER

David Ross

imageplus
publishing

Mindset Before Matter

imageplus publishing

Published by:Imageplus

The Retreat, Sterridge Valley, Berrynarbor, Devon EX34 9TB, England

Telephone: 0845 607 6724

info@imageplus.org.uk

www.imageplus.org.uk

First Edition: 2017 David Ross

Printed in Great Britain by Imageplus, Macclesfield

A CIP catalogue record for this book is available from the British Library
ISBN 978-0-9570506-3-1

THIS BOOK IS DEDICATED TO ALL THE STARSHIP COMMANDERS ON THE PLANET

ABOUT THE AUTHOR

After a background in theatre and the arts, David worked his way up the educational ladder, teaching expressive and performing arts at one of the leading visual arts schools in the UK. In 2004 he went to open one of the largest acting schools in the north-west of England, winning a number of accolades including Business of the Year North West 2008. He went on to eventually license his school as a franchise network opportunity, opening up a number of schools across the UK and helping other educators and teachers achieve greater financial independence.

In 2009 David joined a major British plc network marketing company. Since then he has focused his efforts on growing and developing a large organisation. He has created a strong and positive team and family culture, as well as mentoring and coaching in mindset and team building. He has also become a sought-after speaker and trainer at team events. He regularly interviews and hosts online trainings with top global leaders in the profession, carrying with him a strong belief in providing great value and content to the network marketing community globally. He is well respected both nationally and internationally, and has delivered bespoke trainings to thousands of distributors in various companies in this profession.

In 2015 he was invited by Eric Worre to speak as a rising star in Las Vegas at the Go Pro Recruiting Mastery event, sharing the stage with his heroes Tony Robbins and Bob Proctor. He is the best-selling author of the 2016 book *Mindset Before Matter – For Your Network Marketing Journey*, one of the most gifted books in direct sales as well as being Book of the Month for the UK network marketing community. In 2016 after an influx of training requests, he launched his coaching company The Team Works Coaching. He continues to be a dedicated ambassador for his own company and organisation as well as coaching and mentoring generically for leaders and individuals outside his own business. His latest project focuses on 90-day priming, dedicated to the objective of getting new distributors started the right way and preventing them from quitting early on.

WHAT OTHERS SAY

I first met David in Las Vegas after he attended one of my 'breakthrough' events'. After getting to know him personally, it was clear that he had grown up in a network marketing household and already possessed the foundations to be a great leader. I am proud of what he has achieved in the years since. He is a treasured member of the 'Go Pro' family and I have used his story in a number of my trainings. David has become a great leader and team builder. I know this second installment of his book will speak directly to your new team members.

Eric Worre, founder of Network Marketing Pro, author of GO PRO: 7 Steps To Becoming A Network Marketing Professional

David Ross is theatrical and I mean this in the most positive way! Although he has achieved the highest levels of success in business and network marketing, he brings his love for theatre and drama into his story telling, making this book exciting, compelling, inspirational and instructional. Never boring or dry, David's style will leave you imagining a future with no limits. I'm honored to have been asked to contribute a tiny bit to this fun piece of work. Thank you, David.

Jordan Adler, network marketing millionaire, author of Beach Money, *#1 Earner*

David smashes it out of the park once again in this Sci-Fi sequel to his first book. This exciting next installment of 'Mindset Before Matter' offers a unique experience to the reader. They say 'Don't be better, be different'. David does both in 'How to be a Starship Commander' - Your new team members need to read this book! David clearly understands what it takes to get your ship off the ground and this book can fly you much closer to where you want. Devour it and put it to use!

Todd Falcone, author, speaker and coach, The Fearless Networker

Mindset Before Matter

I have had the opportunity to be in the audience and listen to the passion, wisdom and brilliance of David Ross on several occasions. There were thousands present but I think we all felt like he was talking directly to us. He brought realism and power to his first book 'Mindset Before Matter' and now with this follow up he takes it to a whole new level.

Richard Bliss Brooke, author, **Mach 2 The Art of Vision and Self Motivation, The Four Year Career**

David is an amazing mentor. He is as sincere and authentic a person as you will ever meet and his quiet determination to help others succeed shines through in his book from the very first page. He keeps it simple and methodical so that a brand new person can move right to action and the more experienced person can break through when they hit bumps. A must read for anyone who wants to save time and live free.

Lisa Grossmann, network marketing trainer, million-dollar earner

David just gets it! Every single successful leader has one thing in common. They all have a successful mindset. Without the right mindset nothing else matters. David is a proven leader that has a bulletproof mindset. In this book he teaches the most important techniques to have the right mindset to get your business off the ground. My advice is to not just buy this book but to apply its principles to take you to the next level and share it with your team!

Rob Sperry, Voted 2017 Top Coach by Business for Home, author of **The Game of Networking**

How to be a Starship Commander is a magical follow on from David's first book! It continues to be filled with brilliant and practical insights from a young "been there, done that" network marketing leader who turns around and teaches us what he has learned. Through his own creative imagination, David shows you in a way like no other, how to succeed in network marketing early on. Readers will come away enriched in mindset and inspired to launch their businesses and shoot for the stars!

Dr Josephine Gross, PhD, editor in chief: **Networking Times**

If you are someone that is involved in the network marketing profession that is looking to up your game, I highly recommend checking out David's new book. David is an incredible leader and someone that has a ton of value to offer anyone that's looking to become successful in their business. He's got a servant's heart and a very unique teaching style that makes it both fun and easy to learn.

Bob Heilig, founder of Your Virtual Upline

David's sense of duty to his profession is second to none, there are few Professional Network marketers who can both offer themselves to their own organisation and generically to other companies and maintain the professional balance required to give value to both. I have had the pleasure of spending time with David brainstorming ideas about on how we can be always improving our profession. His unique perspective and approach is always enlightening. He has become a popular choice for guidance and I know his trainings have impacted members of my own team. Get this book read and let's create some more Starship Commanders!

John Holowaty, 7-figure earner, network marketing professional, Go Pro speaker

I have had the pleasure of sharing the stage with David, he is a true gentleman of the profession and represents the network marketing community with integrity and a passion. There are no airs and graces with him. David articulates his ideas in such a way that both your newest team members and the most seasoned professional can relate to them. I have no doubt that this book will present a unique and fun perspective on launching your business!

Hayley Hobson, 7-figure earner, Go Pro speaker

ACKNOWLEDGEMENTS

Thank you to Clive Leach and Diana Ross, who have supported me and my projects: two fantastic life coaches who continue to dedicate their lives to the profession worldwide, their team, and their company. Thank you for keeping our ships on course.

Always in my heart will be Eric Worre and his wife Marina, who gave me the breakthrough I needed at a critical point in my career. I thank you with all my heart for giving me the opportunity to contribute to and become part of your network marketing family.

To Stephan Longworth, Steve Critchley, Wes Linden, Jimmy Chapman and Robin Brooks; thank you for your support. To the Hon. Charles Wigoder, Andrew Lindsay MBE, Wayne Coupland and Paul Goundry, Justin Bozzino and the rest of the amazing team who do a wonderful job and pave the way for us all. To Mark and Angela Jemma James, Andy Wright and Tina Powell and Jane and Darren Turner and the rest of our amazing team for your loyal support.

To so many other phenomenal industry leaders who have inspired me. A special thank you to Jordan Adler for his massive contribution and incredible story.

To Lisa Grossmann, one of the finest trainers I know and a dear friend. To Todd (The Fearless Recruiter) Falcone: thank you for still being the coolest network marketer on Planet Earth. To Richard Bliss Brooke for being an ambassador for our profession. To Samantha Davis, Beth Philips, Katie Hamer, Clare Cowan, Leanne Murphy, Hayley Robinson and Helen Wright, Charlotte Whittle, and Drew Fessenden for supporting the first book!

To Ray and Jessica Higdon, Bob Heilig and Rob Sperry, for sharing awesome content every day.

A big thank you to Jemma James for reviewing the ideas in this book, to Knowledge is King and Alan Hamilton at Imageplus for bringing this book to life.

CONTENTS

THE FUTURE BELONGS TO THOSE WHO SEE OPPORTUNITIES BEFORE THEY BECOME OBVIOUS - JOHN SULLEY

A MESSAGE FROM MISSION CONTROL

Welcome to the Starship Academy, and well done on making it this far. Before we get you suited up, we want you to know that you've already overcome your biggest challenge – that is, making the decision to take this trip. You've made a choice to improve your situation, whatever that may be. You're about to embark on a journey like no other. If you have already studied our first instalment, *Mindset Before Matter – for your Network Marketing Journey*, then you'll be familiar with some of the obstacles you may face over the coming months – but you'll also know what fun and excitement you'll have on this journey. If you haven't read it yet, that's okay; ask your Starship Commander for it, or seek it out yourself.

In this second instalment, *Mindset Before Matter – How to be a Starship Commander*, you will harness the power of the How To? by getting your ship up into the atmosphere in your first 90 days of your business, eventually advancing to our special rank of Starship Commander.

This will be the first part of your journey. The hardest part of any journey is always the beginning. Right here, right now, this is where you can be the most emotionally vulnerable and sometimes the most fearful. At this point, you have made very little emotional investment and the cost of boarding this ship is low, so the temptation for you to turn around and head home will never be far away.

The planets won't align themselves for you. You'll encounter aliens and asteroids that will challenge your mental and physical endurance, and you may start to ask, 'Is freedom really worth it?' Some new recruits like you joining this program don't even make it this far. They don't plug themselves into the learning manuals or, as we like to call it here at the academy, 'personal development'. You'll learn all about that in time. Follow this handbook and your questions will be answered – and we'll give you the opportunity to experience views like no other.

– Starship Commander out

FOREWORD BY JORDAN ADLER

It was 6:00am and I exited the elevator of the Marriott Hotel in Salt Lake City. The Starbucks was inside the hotel and I was the first one at the door prior to their opening. Within the next 30 minutes there would be a line of 50 people waiting to get their morning fix. This was convention week and people had flown in from all over the world to hear the many exciting announcements and to celebrate the successes of the year.

The hotel was quiet and I heard some footsteps echoing through the atrium of the lobby. I turned to see a woman with short red hair walking toward me. She walked right over and said, "Hi, are you Jordan Adler?"

I nodded and she said, "My name is Caroline Ferguson. I'm from Australia." I asked Caroline when she arrived in the United States and also what kind of work she does. She replied that she is a travel agent. I spent many years in the travel industry and had watched this profession fizzle out with the growing accessibility of travel booking websites. Travel agents were becoming obsolete because of the Internet. I believed that most people were now booking their own travel and weren't hiring travel agents too much any more. So I asked Caroline, "How's it going?" fully expecting her to say, "Not too well." But she responded, "Unbelievable! I just had my best year ever in 21 years!" I was floored, and asked her what kind of travel she specializes in. She told me she books "Space". I said, "Space?" And she responds, pointing up

"Yes, space!"

At this point I concluded that Caroline must be booking space in hotel rooms and on cruise ships. She shakes her head, points to the sky and says, "SPACE!!" Now I'm intrigued! She proceeds to tell me that she is a booking agent for one of the first civilian space traveller programs. They plan to begin sending civilians into space by the year 2020 and tickets hold a price tag of $250,000. She had sold four of them.

In the back of my mind, I remembered writing a goal down in a journal about 10 years ago. I remember as I wrote it thinking to myself, "This will never happen!" I was 47 years old and had written down as one of my goals, "Starship Commander" or "Space Traveler". I didn't tell her about it at this moment. I wanted to get home and find the journal that had this goal written in it.

After the convention and returning home to the mountains of Arizona, I began rummaging through boxes looking for my older journals. After skimming through about five of them, there it was ... number 8 on the list. I had written "Space Traveler".

THREE TIMES THE SPEED OF SOUND

About a week later I had an email from Caroline telling me that some of the people running the space program would be in Las Vegas in about a month. She asked me if I would like to meet with them. I said, "Yes, of course!" trying to contain my excitement in my email response.

So three months after meeting Caroline, I met with Rose Kingscote, who works in the office with Richard Branson. She pulled out all the colorful brochures showing me the photos of the spaceships, the space center and the team.

She told me that the trip would take me 100 miles above the earth and that I would get to experience weightlessness, see the curve of the earth and travel 3 times the speed of sound.

I had written down this goal at the age of 47, many years before civilian space travel was even being discussed. On my 57th birthday, I wired $250,000 to become one of the first civilians and network marketers in space.

David's book will take you on a journey to reach your dreams. Although he has used space travel as a metaphor for your very real network marketing journey, this book will cause you to transcend your current reality and build a life that may just be beyond your wildest imagination.

Check out **www.beachmoney.com**

"THE STORIES IN YOUR MIND BECOME
THE STORIES IN YOUR LIFE!"

T -10

MAY THE COURSE BE WITH YOU

IN THE BEGINNING

There are over 7 billion worlds on Planet Earth, because each individual, including you and me, experience a different perspective of reality in accordance with the world that we live in.

All of us on earth live our lives making daily choices and exercising daily habits that will either keep us on the success curve or on the failure curve, while believing in our own perception of what reality actually is. We exist either closer to or further away from objective reality than the people around us, while maintaining varying degrees of self-awareness. That's the shocking truth!

The difference usually depends on several factors: your environment, your social circumstances, your education, your exposure to certain events and situations, and your background and upbringing. Plus all the things that have carved the path of your life until right now: the people you surround yourself with daily, and the things you've chosen to let in and the things that you've chosen to ignore. Plus the opportunities you chose to pass on, and the chances you never took. These are all the sum of what you are today – and if you're truly content, that's okay.

We ask, though, that if you're thinking about joining us on this journey into outer space you consider something: can you accept in this moment and moving forward that *your* reality is not *the* reality? If you can't lock that into your mind from this point, then you may find moving forward difficult; your flight may become disorientated and you may risk getting space dementia.

But if you *can* accept it, then the very best thing that you can be right now is a good student, a Padawan learner, training to venture to a galaxy far, far away and to face head on the aliens and asteroids that will get in your way and will throw you off course if you aren't prepared properly.

Here on earth, it may be the case that something isn't quite working for you ... why else would you be here? A question you must ask yourself is: 'Am I open to accepting that although where I am right now may seem fine in some ways, if I'm moving forward I can't continue to be the same person? Or will I continue to have the same things present in my life?' – That is, the same dramas, the same problems, the same conversations, the same bank balance, the same people in your life and the same journey as everybody else around you in your environment. If you feel okay about keeping all those same things around you, maybe you should stay put, and give this book to someone else.

DO YOU REALLY WANT TO BE A STARSHIP COMMANDER?

Then you've got to get this ship off the ground. You won't achieve this by staying where you are – making those same daily choices and decisions that you've been doing up until now. You need to **have that paradigm shift** and **exchange those daily habits for better ones**. We can show you how to do this in this handbook.

That's what we're here for. We're going to fire up the thrusters beneath you. For the next 90 days, you're going to have to be firing on all cylinders. If you can't make the decision to do this right now, then you may have to **lower your expectations of your life on earth**. This is because what you have in your life will always need to be balanced with what you're prepared to do.

So, what *are* you prepared to do? You have this book in your hands right now. You've made a start, and that can be the hardest part – but you will have to be **prepared to do some things you don't want to do.**

ARE YOU READY TO MAKE A COMITTMENT...?

In a way, it doesn't matter how much time your ship stays in its upright position ready to launch. But the truth is that every single second it spends waiting – waiting for you – it's costing more than you realise. Because waiting is one of the most highly addictive human behaviours to plague our beautiful planet. Many of us love to wait, standing around, hoping for some divine intervention to give us what we want.

If that describes you, then you can see this journey as your divine intervention; right now, there's nothing else you should be focusing on more.

SO PRAY, THEN MOVE YOUR FEET

Wanting it and asking for it, although necessary, is not enough. You can always go back to sleep in the Matrix and simply hope that everything will work out for you –

– or you can take control of your situation and jump onto this ship with all of us. Over the next 90 days we can take off out of this place. It's going be bumpy; you don't get to high places without turbulence and a bit of rough weather.

Make sure you've packed your sick bag; you may need it to tidy up some of that mess you bring – you know, the excuses about how much time you don't have and how you're such a busy person with all the projects and family stuff you have going on, or how your head isn't in the right place. (Though come to think of it, the fact is that most people's heads *aren't* in the right place: they're looking down at the floor instead of looking up to the stars.)

I'm sure that each of the 112 waking hours a week you have available to you are dedicated to meeting your goals and building your wealth plan. If they're not, we can show you how to re-address the balance, to help you feel better. You could most likely pave the way to the moon with all the time you don't think you have. In fact, how much time you have depends on your own personal perspective of time and the activities you engage in. You're here to buy back your time. That's the holy grail of this journey. This is what you've been searching for all this time! This is what everybody around you at the academy is talking about: time freedom, the one true definition of the word 'wealth'.

MONEY YOU CAN MAKE BUT TIME IS GONE FOREVER

This journey won't be easy – you may start to run out of fuel. For example, you'll almost certainly have some people you know and love not wanting you to board this ship. After all, you and they all came from the same place – but unlike you they're too comfortable in the here and now, and the idea of you doing something that goes against what they've previously been taught may go against their own life plan – if, that is, they have one at all. Relax! It's okay, and their resistance is something you should expect. It doesn't mean that the people around you don't love you. It's just that they'll miss you while you're away. Our best advice is: don't concern yourself too much about what others think. Enjoy your journey, do your best and prove to the people in your world that you can be a Starship Commander.

There are some people just like you who've been hoping that an opportunity like this would present itself. You're not the only one with dreams: this is a mission that we can all go on together, and there are many more people you can bring along. But not everybody is going to want to ride in your ship with you. Don't lose faith if the people you love on earth don't want to come with you and they just don't see what you see. Some people want to see what the rocks of Mars look like before they're prepared to actually travel there.

This ship is intended for a one-way trip. We're not interested in returning recruits to their previous life. Make no mistake; this is a life-changing decision for you. It's a one-way journey, so check your baggage allowance. You're going to need to leave some things at home: all your indiscretions, previous successes and failures, wrongdoings and any sense of guilt or lack of worthiness of success. These all need to be left right here on the launch pad. There's neither room nor use for it here. It's extra weight, and it will have no bearing on your success moving forward. Look around you, put it down and don't look back.

We have no use for apologies here.

You have the ship's manual – it's in your hands right now. Check out the picture on the front cover. Go on flip the page – that's you! Read this book, digest it and take it in. Be safe in the knowledge that if used correctly, the information provided will help you **survive your first 90 days**, blast through the atmosphere and hit the rank of Starship Commander. This is not a solo flight: we're an elite team of people and thinkers, and you're part of this team.

You must play your part. We'll help you, but it's your responsibility to ensure that your part of the mission goes according to plan.

In return, your team will support and guide you.

On earth, you have believed that you were worth more than you had been given credit for. In the next 90 days, we'll see if you were right.

Your ship awaits!

T -9

PRE-LAUNCH MISTAKES

Okay, are you ready for what's next? Let's discuss what you need to avoid before you go on board. Here are some in-flight guidelines to keep you on course over the next 90 days of your mission.

Recruits just like you joining this program have often found themselves making the same mistakes time and again. Here at the academy it's our job to protect you **and get you started the right way** so we can be sure that you don't repeat the mistakes of those who have come before you. Keeping your initial launch on the correct trajectory and successfully breaking through the atmosphere can often determine the success of your entire journey. Try to relax and have fun. This is a time to celebrate, so we want you to log the following information into your database, to have it to hand when you need it. This will assist you at all times in making sure you avoid any of these actions and behaviours.

1. DON'T BE A CRUSADER

You've **made the choice** to take this journey, and this is to be commended. It doesn't, however, make you an expert, or for that matter wiser than anybody else around you. Choose caution and avoid placing your ideals and beliefs onto everyone you know. You may just alienate them in the process. Aliens can be very difficult to handle, as you'll discover later on in this handbook.

You may have seen the light, you may be excited about changing the world and travelling into outer space and beyond the stars. That's great! You may have just come to the realisation that you have something that can save the world from certain destruction, and now this amazing opportunity can save the people of earth from the bondage of society and certain doom when the asteroid hits.

All the amazing things that you will have learned so far about your mission … be careful not impart all this information to those closest to you. People on earth don't like too much information too soon, as you will come to learn as we move on.

Mindset Before Matter

The people in your environment and those closest to you **are not likely to be particularly interested in your journey to the stars**. This can be a hard pill to swallow when you're full of excitement. Who wouldn't be, after all? They're not overly concerned about how beautiful your ship is, and they certainly don't want you to tell them that they need your help. Most people don't want to be helped, because they believe that they're fine just the way they are. Nice and cosy! For them, this planet is fine just the way it is, and their reality is *the* reality.

Moving upward and onwards, we want to show you how people make decisions. This will be the key to avoiding many of the pre-launch mistakes. It will also give you more power than you can possibly imagine. Once you harness the knowledge and understanding of how people behave, you'll be well on your way to becoming a Starship Commander.

We can help position you so that **people won't ignore you**. You can and will get to a point where people will take your advice so that you can effectively help them. This will happen mostly when they need you. Your first real lesson is to understand that although you may think that people need your help and advice – and they most likely will at some point – it needs to be on their terms and **only when they're ready to receive it**.

You may have heard the old expression, 'Don't wait till you're thirsty to dig your well.' But although we like teaching people that **prevention is better than cure** – a great sentiment – human beings simply don't behave that way. It's one of the things that separate us from the animal kingdom on earth. We're not good at preparing for a crash landing.

Whatever problem you're helping the world to solve, **people are most likely to listen to you** when they're experiencing an actual problem, or when they sense that a crash landing is imminent in their own lives.

Some animals are very good at preparation and prevention. They can anticipate impending problems, situations and changing seasons. They can make decisions and take actions to prevent an unwanted or undesirable outcome. But although some early humans were like that, most of the people you know on earth now are simply not built that way. They want the problem to happen first. They want to be in pain before they come to you for a cure. **Your greatest prospect** is the one who needs you.

When people tell you they're happy just where they are and that they're happy with what they have, what they're saying is that they're not unhappy enough to do something about it. They're comfortable enough with their situation in life. You have most likely felt this way yourself at some point. Many people are not mentally positioned to make the decision that **you can see would be advantageous for them to make** because of this. People can often **struggle to make the decisions that improve their situation**, which is why so many people you know on earth are suffering when they don't need to.

It's not about you. You can help guide people to a decision – but it's important that you remove your emotion from the outcome. Don't make yourself the issue. **The timing of people's decisions is way more important than your ego**.

2. DON'T WASTE YOUR TICKET

You signed up for this mission. You have your ticket to fly to the stars, but bear in mind that this isn't a lottery ticket. You have most likely invested and paid a registration fee to board this ship. This doesn't entitle you to any kind of reward. The only thing your fee entitles you to is support and training – which is exactly what you're going to get here at the academy. Maybe you were given some goodies in the starter pack which came with your sign-up, but essentially what you have in your hands right now is a boarding pass. So hold onto it with pride!

You have purchased a **course in personal development** and self-discovery. **There is a business opportunity attached to it**, and you will be provided with the same tools and controls that were given to every other Starship Commander who came before you.

Nobody's going to fly this ship for you. You will have the controls. You'll take the control column for the next 90 days and beyond. The downside of this means that you can turn the ship around at any time you like. For so many recruits who enter into this program, **there is a very low cost of entry but perhaps more dangerously, a low emotional investment**. Many new recruits signed up to the mission simply because it seemed like a good idea at the time.

But most of the launches that have been successful have taken years of preparation and planning. How long have you been considering taking this trip? If it's not that long, this means that it will be incredibly easy for you to head home when things don't go your way. Blasting through is the only thing that can reward you – and with a ride like this you'll get some casualties, but they won't be your own. You don't need to be one of them; you can be different! If your expectations are realistic from the beginning and you're prepared to handle the bumps that come with a trip of this nature, you can have practically anything you want.

EVEN THE STARS!

The big question you need to ask yourself is how do you value this mission? If you bought your own ticket, it wasn't for a lot of money, but you still paid! So …

Do you value this mission at the price of its entry, or do you value it at the price of what it could provide for you in the long term? Do you see where it could take you in the future? If it's the latter, then you're on the way to being a Starship Commander. But if you're still obsessing over what it cost you to get in, then **you'll need to report to the sick bay for some mindset conditioning**. Don't panic! – it's not going to hurt, and all new recruits must go through it at some point. We'll be heading there later.

3. WE DON'T NEED YOUR CREDENTIALS

We know that you've worked hard to get where you are up until the point of joining this mission. You should be proud that you've survived the rat race on earth this far. It's clear you've earned some recognition and have achieved some things in the last few decades that you can be proud of. We don't want to discount any of those achievements you've already acquired, and we expect you to use your personality and character to your advantage on this mission. Many new recruits at the academy stop being human at the beginning of their journey, so much so that the ones they know and love can sometimes fail to recognise them. You're here through your own choice, a choice you've made. Your current behaviour tells the story of where you've been, but it has absolutely no bearing on where you are headed.

At the academy you will speak to many of our Starship Commanders who have no formal qualifications. They have worked their way up the ranks through hard work and true grit, all with varying degrees of ambition and success. These are people you need to stay close to. They can protect you during dangerous parts of the mission. For once in your life, right here, right now, you have the chance to get to the top, irrespective of your past. Whatever previous successes and failures you have encountered, you need to leave them right here on the launch pad. This is baggage you don't want to bring on this trip. There's no room for it.

4. WHO MIGHT YOU TAKE WITH YOU?

Consider all the people who've been around you for years when you embark on this journey. Friends, family, people you know, and people you've met previously. A standard pre-launch error for some recruits is convincing yourself that you know very few people who would want to help you or even join you on your journey.

At the beginning, right now, it's important to look at the big picture. The correct process for moving forward is to think of everybody you know, rather than only listing all the people who you believe may want to join you.

It's not your job to cherry-pick a few individuals, but rather to issue an invitation to everybody you know to share in this amazing journey.

At check-in, your Starship Commander should sit down with you and ask you to provide them **with a list of all your contacts**. If they haven't, they should do this with you at pre-launch. Speak to them about it. We'll expand on this and give further advice later in this book. It's important to know from the off that a good list doesn't separate those people you feel you want to invite along from everybody you know.

5. BOTTOM OF THE PILE

At the academy, Starship Commanders can get frustrated when they see a new recruit make a sudden shift in priorities once they have boarded the ship, because this change of mind can be dangerous, leading to failure. You need to sustain the excitement and commitment both pre and post launch. Where have you placed the importance of this mission on your own personal priority list?

For the next 90 days, this mission should be your number one priority. As a rule of list making, you should always be prioritising the things that will reward you years down the line, while placing those things that may be urgent today or in the moment at the bottom of your pile. Don't wake up on a daily basis and look at the stars in the sky above, worrying about what needs to be done today. You should be concerning yourself with the activity that's going to pay you in the future.

Note that looking up and aiming up are two different things. You must at all times **place the important before the urgent.** Think for a moment about how most people on earth are getting through each day: slaves to the moment, to the cooking, to picking kids up, to keeping the boss happy, to picking up the dry cleaning, to walking the dog and everything else they deem to be important.

These things may seem important. But they're *not* important – they're urgent. You need to be prioritising the choices and decisions that may not satisfy you today but trust that they will give you abundance in years to come. **Don't place this mission at bottom of the pile just because there is no immediate reward today**. So many of the people on earth live day to day, surviving in an existence that will never reward them, never get them to where they want to be, because they are trying to manage the time they don't believe they have on a daily basis. What you should be doing differently is prioritising the activities you need to do each day that are aimed at creating long-term success and happiness. Those activities are not the urgent matters you need to attend to, so don't confuse yourself.

Before you hit 'stasis' each night, make a list of everything that needs to get done the next day. At the top of your list, place everything that will benefit you in five years time. Think about this long and hard. If you dont know how to do this, speak to your Starship Commander. At the bottom of your list, place everything that needs to get done that day, the urgent things. This shift in prioritising will affect not only the outcome of your next 90 days but also the entire lifetime of your journey. You will also become less resentful towards the things you feel are a drain on your time. Because when you only concern yourself with what needs to be done to survive today there is no future.

Dont make the mistake of taking comfort in tomorrow because tomorrow is a fictional place. You can never get there; it only exists in your headspace. What you need to do today and will place you where you need to be on this mission in five years time needs to be clearly distinguished. Make your first list tonight. Use the space at the back of this handbook.

6. GETTING "ALL SINATRA"

Back in the mid-20th century, Frank Sinatra recorded a great song called 'My Way'; it was about a man looking back fondly on a life he'd lived on his own terms. This is rather poignant, and lends itself to one question: Can you live life doing things your way and live on your own terms? Evidence suggests that you can't. Not until you've earned the right to do so. **You can't** *have* **what you want and** *do* **what you want at the same time – not, that is, until you've earned it.** The problem is that **most people have the poor mindset that they deserve.** That's because their expectations in life far outweigh what they're prepared to do to meet those expectations. It's paradoxical.

I want you to think about this mission and its success. If you want to smash through the atmosphere up into space, can you achieve this by doing it your way? Are you likely to achieve success by re-writing the rules to suit you? Or … are you more likely to run a successful mission by following the guidance of a Starship Commander and others who have already been successful at the very thing you want to achieve?

If you reckon so, that means doing it somebody else's way, going against the grain of what your previous habits and learned behaviour dictate, which is to stay safe and comfortable. In brief, **if you want to do something you've never done before and want to be successful, you'll have to do some things you don't want to do!** Scary thought. But in fact if you can acquire this mode of thought you'll have so much fun! Doing things you don't want to do and moving out of your comfort zone will give you a huge sense of progress. That is the high that you seek! It's kind of like a drug.

T -8

WELCOME TO SICKBAY

Welcome to sickbay! Now that we've set out some expectations for behaviour, it's time to administer what we call a Flu Jab. Here at the academy we like to have fun with our recruits, and while **understanding what to avoid is a great first step,** we have some serious questions we need to ask you, in order to check your suitability for flight. Space dementia is serious; we don't want you doing something daft up there like quitting, so it's necessary for us to administer five quick flu jabs to help you with this early part of the mission. Don't worry, it doesn't hurt; in fact we think you'll find it a very interesting exercise.

Your behaviour on this program and on this trip can affect everybody around you. While all recruits are ultimately responsible for their own choices, we have a responsibility to support you and those around you, to ensure you're safe and can make the most of this amazing opportunity.

DID YOU BRING A SICKBAG?

No, we didn't think so. Every recruit forgets. It's okay; we have one right here. Before we shortly board the ship, each recruit must go through a quick heath check. We need to take a closer look and examine you. It's important that we firstly root out any issues concerning poor learned behaviour or any unresolved trauma you may be bringing with you on this trip. This could affect things moving forward. That's why we have to administer these flu jabs.

Our task in sickbay is to help you let go of any outdated thoughts or previous ideas that may affect your ability to fly this ship. Please understand that we're not saying that you're sick, but for space flight, a mental health check is necessary to ensure you can make the most of it and don't risk the safety of those around you.

PAY ATTENTION OR PAY THE PRICE

This is not a cure. There's nothing wrong with you – it's simply a preventative measure designed to give you the best possible start so you can go into this with your eyes wide open. Clarity of vision, as you would expect with this kind of mission, is very important. Some recruits in the past have quit this program **simply because they were not paying attention to what was going on around them**; they couldn't see correctly, their vision was blurred. So our first and best piece of advice at this point is pay attention to what's going on on board and in your general surroundings.

It's easy to allow yourself to get left behind, so **flu jab#1** is to protect you from this. Most of the information you require to become a successful Starship Commander will not be brought to you on a silver plate, although this handbook has all you need for a successful launch. You must get great at being proactive and seeking out information. **If you don't have a heightened sense of awareness, both of yourself and what is happening in your new environment, you'll miss things**. This is a self-service mission. We will help you – but we won't do it for you.

WHY AM I HERE?

Perhaps the biggest question all new recruits will be asked on Day One, and a question you should ask yourself is: Why am I here?

What are your exact reasons for boarding this ship? This will be without a doubt the most important defining question in establishing your suitability for flight. The truth is that for far too many new recruits, it just seemed like a good idea at the time. If this is the case, there is a good chance you may struggle over the next 90 days. You may be tempted to turn around and head back home – and that's not really an option, so it needs to be fixed. But if you're a recruit who has decided from the heart to make this journey with a strong attachment to something, or a desire level with close personal reasons, then you'll be among the strongest candidates, and one most likely to succeed.

Flu jab#2 should help you explore your WHY? power for being here. Is your reason for being here a big enough one for you to step out of your comfort zone? The problem with being here because the price of entry is small and the benefits of joining seem to outweigh the losses is that it moves you away from any real purpose, and so this exercise becomes a gamble.

Mindset Before Matter

The expectations you tell us about will most likely not be met. If you're anything like most recruits, you will lie to us ...

... and that's because most, if not all, new recruits are over-inflated when it comes to letting us know their desire levels – that is, telling us how far they really want to go on this journey.

This is why some new recruits end up flying back home. We can't imagine, though, that you'd want to be one of them: whatever you're missing in your life, this journey can give you the tools to fill that gap. It can provide you with a vehicle to satisfy your wants, needs and desires. So you need to spend some time to figure out what's missing in your life and decide if it's worth working for.

Flu jab#3 will help you to be realistic at this point about what you can expect from signing up to this program. This next jab is particularly important **because it can preserve the relationships you need to maintain with your Starship Commander** and those around you. This is necessary in order to achieve your goals. Recruits can often break away from, fall out with, stop speaking to or stop working with their supporting officer. This usually happens **because they're being pulled in a direction they dont truly want to go** – and *that* happens because they havent been honest at the beginning about their desire levels. Similarly if youre new, dont let your Starship Commander try to pull you in a direction you currently don't want to go. Yes, some Starship Commanders can sometimes, with the best intentions in the world, try to create you in their own image. They mean well, but you must be honest about your own desires. This preserves great working relationships when youre miles above the atmosphere.

There are three key elements to your expectations on this trip:

1. What you want and desire.

2. What you're prepared to do to get it.

3. What you feel you deserve.

You'll almost certainly be faced early on with a conflict between these three elements. This is because much of the learned behaviour some recruits bring on board is **I want and I deserve** without any thought for how they will achieve it. Worse, many recruits don't really know what they want; they just know they want more than they currently have. They have no plan, and no idea what they want, but they feel sure that they deserve more than they have.

Can you see why so many people aren't happy with their situation back on earth? Go and take a quick break right now. Go away and think about this before you move forward. Write your thoughts down in the notes section of this handbook. Test yourself: do you really know what you want from all of this? If you don't, you need to address it. Read on!

If you wish to preserve the relationships with the people who are helping you on this mission, you need to be honest from the start about what it is you really want. Don't exaggerate: don't tell your Starship Commander you want to earn £2,000 per month if you're only prepared to work at a £7 an hour mentality, or that you want a millionaire lifestyle when your work ethic will net you £1,000 per month. This is why in the early stages of launch you may have to lower your desire levels to match what you're prepared to do. This way you won't be guided to a place so far out of your comfort zone that you crash-land early on.

This is very important. Be honest from the start and know your earning potential in conjunction with your work ethic. Never increase your wants or desire levels without expecting to work harder and to be taken to a place further out of your comfort zone by those who are trying to help you achieve what you want. This realisation is your responsibility. If you're uncomfortable at any point, this is probably okay, and can be expected as you're pushing boundaries – but it may also be an indication that you don't want the change badly enough, so you may need to pull back on the controls, that is, reduce your expectations of what you're aiming for.

Of course we want you to be the best you possibly can be, so our advice to you is to **summon up a bigger reason for being here**. If the reason and desire are big enough, then the discomfort will ease and help you put pedal to metal. So we ask you one last time: Why are you here?

MISPLACED FOCUS

From birth, you've been programmed for survival. **But *survival* and *living* are two planets a million miles apart**. We can teach you how to live – that is, how to be happy each day and how to enjoy the ride – but it will go against the grain of your previous belief systems.

Flu jab#4 will give you some clarity on why you may be dissatisfied, and give you a better understanding of why many people you know could be feeling the same. It's all down to a misplaced focus. Surviving in the real world means not being uncomfortable enough to change your habits in order to live the way you want. Find me some people you know from your contacts list on earth who put their goals and plans before their work and interests: you may be able to count them on one hand.

This is why so many people from all walks of life and backgrounds are dissatisfied with their lack of journey. The only way I know of that you can be truly happy as an individual is **if you feel you're progressing or getting better**. Whether it's health, wealth or relationships, it's not so much the severity or state that matters; if you don't feel you're progressing or getting better it can start to have a negative effect.

Think about what gets you down. You rarely have ongoing negative thoughts because of a single event. What gets you down is mostly a lack of events taking place that are improving your situation. **It's what's *not* happening that so often feeds hopelessness**. Even if this is not you right now, there is a basic human need for growth in most people at certain stages of life. Just like a young plant finding its niche in the natural world, we need to grow, we want to grow! But progress can't be achieved **if you consistently put your work and your interests before your goals and your plans**! Remember what we discussed earlier about your priority list.

What's more, even if you do have a goal, with no plan it's just a dream.

So the answer to happiness is to have a goal with a plan that will eventually get you there. **You don't have to give up the things you need to do as part of your life and your routine**. Your job and your hobbies, they're all fine – but you need to readdress the balance and shift your focus onto the long term rather than believing that your immediate interests and your long-term goals can't co-exist. If you don't place a high value on something such as this mission that *doesn't* create an instant fix today, then chances are you'll end up not finding the time for it.

If you're not working towards being in a better position than you're in right now, you'll remain discontented, unless you're a cyborg. With our help, your plan is not difficult to create. Ask your Starship Commander to talk through this with you. All the information provided in this book maps out what you need to do to break through the atmosphere, so we have provided an initial plan for you.

The best way to form any plans in life is to begin with what you truly want. Be honest first – don't lie, either to us or to yourself – and figure out what you want, what you're aiming for. Then work backwards through the steps you need to get you to that point. We call it reverse engineering. Too many people try to work forwards, but this is hard because they don't know where they're going.

You need to make a plan *now*! Without one you will run your ship on autopilot, which is programmed to avoid the asteroid fields – but it's in the danger zone where success lies.

HOW IMPORTANT ARE OTHER PEOPLES OPINIONS?

Most of us have spent an eternity dancing to the beat of other people: we place so much stock in what other people tell or advise us that it often is a large contributing factor to our choice, and what they tell us is often where we end up.

Flu jab#5 should give you more control over your own choices and decisions. How many people have told you or encouraged you to board this ship and shoot for the stars? Not many! Remember this: if lots of people are telling you to do something, or perhaps not to, **doing what they say will take you to an average place – and you didn't sign on to this program to be average.**

When people feed you their opinions on the decisions you should make, this is usually based on what suits *them* best emotionally, and you feel obliged to indulge them. You can end up making decisions that keep others happy and prevent those around you from behaving negatively, so your choices are more about prevention than determination. This is a failure-curve mentality.

Mindset Before Matter

There are going to be people who are unhappy about your decision to take this journey towards being a Starship Commander. There will be people who question your reasoning for embarking on this incredible mission. There may even be a few people who think the whole thing is ridiculous. Know that the problem is not with you; it's with them. You have nothing to do with what they think and say, although it may feel that way at the time. So you must fight the urge to fit in with their needs.

Nobody is qualified to advise on your mission other than those who are on the mission with you, and **nobody should be more excited than you about your mission**!

Now you have your flu jabs, it's time for a bit of fun – the bit that all new recruits like to get stuck into. Let's get you tooled up, because it's nearly time to go!

WEAPONS TRAINING

It's the bit you've been waiting for! You're about to get a crash course in the key weapons that will be made available to you over the next 90 days. These can be used to help keep you safe. Please note that these weapons are not to be used for attack, nor are they designed to harm any individual directly. The following weapons are at your disposal, but they're nothing more than tools to help you inform and educate people while you make your journey. These weapons will liberate you, will provide safe and effective exposure (see below) for the people you know, and will provide greater knowledge and understanding to those around you about your journey. These weapons have been designed to help others make an informed decision as to whether they want to help you or even join you as a new recruit on this mission.

Each weapon is incredibly powerful in its own right. You will most likely find that each one will need to be used multiple times, and sometimes you will need to use each weapon more than once. But occasionally you may only need to use a particular weapon once for success. Either way, the weapons provided are all designed by some very smart Starship Commanders, and they're proven to work in your favour. When the time comes, you'll know how to use each weapon, so don't overly concern yourself right now with implementation – when the time comes you'll know what to do. This is because over time you will learn how to use each weapon so that you can maximise its effectiveness.

Note, too, that some weapons, if not handled correctly, may not work to your advantage. Some can be very destructive to your ship! Weapons are only safe if you know how to use them correctly. Your Starship Commander should be able to assist you with this, and walk you through step by step on how these weapons can be effectively used by you on behalf of the company backing your mission.

There will be some weapons and additional items you'll need to seek out yourself, so you must be proactive at obtaining information. Don't just sit on the launch pad waiting to be handed these weapons. As you advance, in time and certainly after 90 days, you may even, with the permission of your company and Starship Commanders, start to craft your own weapons - great fun! Some recruits who are serious about their mission have done this very successfully.

Please take the time to familiarise yourself with each one individually and understand its application. If you're unsure of anything, then please make some notes and refer to your Starship Commander for assistance.

We often refer to your weapons as **'exposures'**. We find it helps to use this term as it primes your mind for using them correctly. For many years, some recruits just like you have successfully used these exposures in order to provide the people with the information they need to jump on board.

You should be using your weapons frequently in this important time frame. You will learn about this just before you launch.

In this section, T -7, we'll break down each weapon and give you a comprehensive look at how it can work for you on your journey. Please be aware that some weapons work better in a certain order, so take that into account in your choices.

Are you ready to take the next step and to explore the hardware you have available to you on your mission?

1. THE SIZZLER

The entry-level weapon, and weapon of choice for most recruits embarking on this journey, is the Sizzler. This will be a video or audio presentation that has been made available to you by your Starship Commander and the company backing your mission. It's a brief video or audio presentation that has been especially designed to present information about the company you're partnered with. This is a fantastic and handy tool for you to quickly and effectively invite people you know to find out more about your journey. The secret to using this weapon effectively is to use it *after* permission has been given to you by the person you want to invite to look.

The single biggest error made by recruits is that they start firing off this weapon at everybody they know without warning them – bullets flying everywhere. This is a grave error, and you will almost certainly hurt lots of people and alienate them to a point where there may be no coming back. Never *ever* use this weapon without permission from the person you want to see it.

The Sizzler is a great way to present your business to people you know. It should provide them with enough information to either make a decision to join or to help you, or at least to gain a level of interest so they can take another look. You have full control over this weapon and how you use it. It has easy access and it's very practical. You can keep to hand and use it on the fly or even send it to people who are in a different location from you. It's incredibly versatile and can reach long distance. You know what to expect each time you use it. It's what we at the academy call very 'duplicatable'. If you've not yet been shown how to access this tool, make a note now, and be sure that you have access to it today. If your company doesn't provide you with this tool, then with their permission and our help you may be able to craft your own.

This is both a long-distance and short-range weapon. Be sure that you maintain good posture when using it at close range. Your job here is to show, not to convince. So, with those people you know well, you may wish to try the following:

"Hey, I'm really excited! I've just started a new business, as I've decided to branch out. I have a short video presentation. Would you do me a favour and take a quick look? I'd really value your feedback. There may be something in for you, too."

People will react differently to this weapon. Some may wish to help you by becoming a customer. Others may wish to join you on your journey as a new recruit. Some may have more questions, in which case you will be able to use other weapons as described below in this chapter. Many will have no interest at all – and that's okay, so be sure to expect this.

2. THE ROOM

Perhaps the most powerful of all the weapons. This too can be a short- and a long-range weapon, but it does work better at short range. The Room can be best described as a **local meeting or event.** Your Starship Commander or the person supporting you should be able to provide you with more information about which meetings and events are available to you in your local area or even at a distance. **We suggest that you fill your diary over the next 90 days with all the meetings and events that are taking place** in your area so you're fully aware of what's going on.

The Room can also be used long range in the form of national seminars, so that people who haven't yet joined your mission can still come along.

Bringing someone you know to a meeting or event to meet other people who also represent your company, is a powerful way to validate the reality of your journey and your mission. There is a huge social currency with the Room as new people get to hear the stories from other recruits like you, who are embarking on a similar mission. This gives extra, third-party, credibility to your mission and reinforces what it is that you're trying to achieve. **The power of association is fundamental to introducing people you know to the other people on the same mission as you**. This makes it more real.

Later on this book we will discuss how **stories are your ultimate social currency** on this journey.

The Room will probably be the most powerful tool available to you. It can sometimes be a slightly more difficult weapon to use because you will be largely relying on the cooperation of the person you're inviting to turn up. **Understanding how to create excitement and urgency**, and understanding how to get a commitment from your guest is key. As powerful as this weapon is, it can only be used in short bursts. This means there may not always be an event or local meeting available at the time you want. This is why using this as an exposure works well after you have used the Sizzler, though this is not always necessary. You may just wish to get your contact – maybe more than one – into the room before anything else: after all, if they are serious and interested they will show up.

In the decision-making process, human beings can struggle with commitment. While it may be easy for somebody you know to agree to attend a meeting or seminar with you, **don't be surprised if on the day of the event they cancel on you**. In most cases, whatever story they feed you with for not attending, it will almost certainly not be the truth. The reality is, that they are simply struggling to be honest about the fact that what seemed a good idea a week ago doesn't seem like such a good idea on the day. It's normal human behaviour – and you'll almost certainly have done it too. As human beings generally like to avoid confrontation they can be dishonest about their feelings. Most of us will mask what we are really feeling with a story – a story which will justify them in being a no show or not participating. This is a behaviour that you too will be tempted to use on your mission – but always be honest about your feelings.

And don't take anything personally.

If you wish to reduce the number of times people don't turn up to events or seminars may we suggest a strategy? If you want somebody you know to attend a meeting or seminar that you have invited them to, then we have a tip for you:

Explain to them that there is a smart casual dress code (no spacesuits). Tell them that you'll book and check them in, and that you've told people all about them and they're really excited to meet them.

This makes the event more real to them, and harder to back out of. It's not real unless you tell them this. To top it off, if it's a small local meeting you can arrange to pick them up and drop them off; this way you'll eliminate any excuses regarding travel. You won't believe how many vehicles break down on the way to an event.

Then, on the way to the event or indeed at the event, the last thing you should be doing is talking about the business or the mission. Talk about their day and what's going on in their lives. When you have arrived at the event with your guest, one of the most powerful things you can do is connect your guest with a like-minded person. Seek out a Starship Commander who knows the etiquette of how to behave at an event. If you can seek out a leader who has a mutual interest with your guest, this is perfect. In space talk we call it **mutual window dressing**.

Let go of your ego. Your friend is more likely to join on the basis of what a third-party person or third-party story tells them, as opposed to what you have to say. They may not see you as the expert – they see you as their friend.

So...

"I'm really excited, I've just started a new business as I'm branching out, and I have a short presentation on Tuesday evening. Would you come along and give me some feedback? I'd really value that. We can grab a drink. I'll pick you up and drop you off."

3. THE MENTOR

The third weapon in the pack, and perhaps the most underused in your armoury, is the Mentor. What's so wonderful about this weapon is that it combines the power of the Sizzler and the power of the Room with the added bonus of being accessible at any point. However, many find it a psychologically difficult weapon to use. This is because it may feel unnatural; however, if you take advantage of this awesome weapon, it can help you recruit people in their dozens onto your journey.

On your journey, you should have been introduced to a friend or somebody you know or have met, perhaps even a Starship Commander in your company, as your sponsor, recruiter or mentor, however you see them. Either way you should have access to somebody who's currently had more success than you. If you don't, add this to your to do list. First, you need to go and seek them out. Do you know their story? This is very important, and you should make the effort to find this person today.

You should have a contact that is supporting you, somebody who knows more about this mission and journey than you do. You can expect this individual, whoever they may be, to talk to all your potential new recruits. What you have here is the added bonus of a local event, because your prospect gets to speak to a third-party expert, somebody other than you. Also this weapon works great at long distance, as you can easily arrange for your mentor to speak to your prospects, no matter where they are on the planet. Your mentor is able to speak to your prospects in a way that you cannot. This is fundamentally important because if you're going to be introducing people you know to this journey, it's also important to know their reasons, their hopes, their goals and what they want to achieve and get out of it. When you have such a close relationship or strong connection with the people on your contacts list, it can often be difficult to speak to them directly in this way.

This is why **connecting people you know** with **whoever is supporting you** is a great way to get people jumping on board.

You're going to have to become most skilled with this weapon.

You're going to have to learn the story of your mentor. How did they get involved with this journey in the beginning, and how did they become successful? Sharing this information with the people that you know is critical if you're going to get them to connect. Think of it a little bit like a reference. You're asking somebody of standing to get in touch with people you know to give them reinforcement about something.

In the real world, we call **this third-party edification**. This is simply the **act of you saying something nice about another individual who's helping you** so that you can connect them with another person you know. This is not a new idea; people on earth, including you, have been doing this since time began. This weapon should always be used to get the questions of your prospect answered as opposed to information simply being hurled their way. Get good at making times for your contacts to speak with your mentor!

This is a skill that you can use to help you on your mission.

So ...

"Can I make a time to get them to call you? They're fantastic, and they're helping me get started. They've been incredibly successful! This is their story ..."

Or ...

"Can I quickly get them on the phone for you? They'll explain it better than I can."

4. THE DIAL IN

Depending on the company you're partnered with, you may or may not have this weapon at your disposal. What you will generally find is that **most companies have some kind of dial-in conference call**, which allows you to use your phone to listen to a presentation. This may either be live or pre-recorded, depending on your company setup. This is a great tool for on-the-fly prospecting as you can use it almost immediately, whether you're with your prospect or not. This will allow your prospect to hear some condensed information about the business and the mission, and also hear some of the stories from other people who have achieved success. This is powerful stuff! It's important to ask your Starship Commander at the academy, or whoever introduced you, if your company provides a dial-in conference so you can share it with the people you know. They can often work well as a first exposure to the business, and if you're with somebody you can simply dial in on your phone so you know they've listened. Dial-in gives you great control and flexibility to involve people you know, but also you're safe in the knowledge that it's always giving the correct information.

This has been used for years, and is one of the earliest weapons to be used on this mission. Make sure you find out if you have access to this.

So ...

"Would you do me a favour and just have a quick listen to this and give me some feedback? There may be something in for you!"

5. THE BOOK

This weapon is very effective, but only on certain people. It can be best described as a book, document or magazine which explains your business. This may be a company-related document – that is, one specific to the company you're partnered with – or it may be a generic document which talks about your mission, much like this book.

You may have been given this book to read before you joined this mission. It's very powerful, but you should in turn only give it to an individual who has the predisposition and positive mental attitude and character to actually read what you have given them. This weapon is often best not to be used as the first exposure. It is at its most powerful when somebody has actually joined and signed up to the mission, rather than using it as a weapon to get them on board. Call it a post-joining exposure. This is how you're most likely using it right now.

Once an individual has joined, personal development books are going to play a large part of their journey. I commend you for reading this book, because right now you have a powerful weapon in your hand. Personal development is fundamental to the growth of your business and the success of your journey. Self- education through books and other training material will be absolutely key if you wish to become a leader at the academy. At the back of this book we have provided you with some fantastic resources for material you can use.

6. THE WEBINAR

The webinar is the most recent of all the weapons available and is becoming more popular as the weapon of choice, particularly amongst the younger generation of recruits joining the program. It has made room for many cultural changes we have started to see since the beginning of the 21st century. If your program is very much social media based, then you will most likely see this weapon being used daily. Some people at the academy call them online parties, and they work particularly well for new recruits launching their business for the first time. Once you board your ship in T -5, you may be able to combine the information you receive with this weapon: it could make for an effective and speedy launch. This is something you should discuss with your Starship Commander, as you will most likely need somebody who's had experience in using this weapon to show you how to use it correctly.

"I'm really excited, I've just started a new business as I'm branching out, and there is a quick webinar on Tuesday evening explaining more. Would you log on and give me some feedback?"

7. THE HOME

This can be one of the best methods. The Home, like the Dial-in, is one of the first, maybe even the first ever, weapon to be used in launching a ship. This weapon is a mixed bag. Only some people can use it successfully, and few will truly master it. If you do get to grips with this weapon, it can give you more exponential growth than any of the other weapons put together. This may be a weapon you want to use in conjunction with T -5 when you board your ship.

The Home gives you the ultimate power to bend time and space. If your mission is to show to 30 people, one by one, in 90 days, then that would take around 30 hours of presentation time. But if you're lucky enough to have a home, a command centre, into which you can fit 30 people, then that's one hour of presentation time for 30 people.

This is also an exceptional weapon for building locally and driving momentum into those thrusters. If you have support, you should invite your Starship Commander or somebody helping you to come along and present to the people you know. You could even host your own, and use your Sizzler videos to present the information to everybody. How easy would that be?

If you're in a position to achieve this, then we strongly urge you to do so. You can even support your new recruits in doing the same!

Mindset Before Matter

Finally, if you haven't done so already we would like to suggest that one of the first things you do is go and seek out as many weapons as you can and establish the level of support you have.

"I'm really excited, I've just started a new business as I'm branching out, and I am having a launch party on Tuesday evening. Would you come along and support me? I'd really value that."

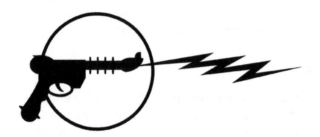

T -6

SKILLS SCHOOL

Almost time to board the ship, but before you get behind that control panel and take over the control column, we have to put you through skills school. The time is getting close, so we need to make sure that you're fully equipped before you jet off to the deep beyond!

This is not a test and there's no exam. **There is no pass or fail** with this part of the induction at the academy. DO NOT let the word 'school' throw you. Many of the lessons you've previously learned in life are okay – but where you're going, you won't need them. Don't obsess over learning everything straight away. Knowledge seeking is fine – but knowledge is gained over a lifetime and not compacted into 90 days, so don't try it. Let go of the need to know it all, and have fun! As long **as you can push buttons and be excited** and be mindful of what we've taught you here, you're set up to do well.

The skills we're about to cover in this section of the book will take you years to perfect, so relax. This is a crash course, so that you *don't* crash over the next 90 days! To be successful on this mission, you don't need to be great at all of the skills. We find many recruits have varying degrees of skill and understanding when it comes to each skill set. You may be great at some of them without even knowing it yet!

We'll break down each skill and explain where it fits into the process and how important each skill is to the growth of your business and the successes of the mission you're about to embark on. Don't panic! As we've explained, in the early stages of your mission, you'll rely mostly on your excitement and urgency rather than following the general human belief that you have to be an expert before you can move. After all babies fall over many, many times before they can walk – and you and I have been through that process and succeeded.

This not to say that these skills should be discounted in any way, because you're going to have to start using them immediately. Just don't spend too long trying to get your head around everything. If you do, it could result in failure to launch. Too many recruits are still standing right here on the launch pad after so much time. **Take a look around and you can see them!** That's not acceptable. An emphasis on knowledge seeking in the early days can be crippling. Knowledge is **important, but not fundamental** to your early success.

People looking to join you on this mission will be drawn to your excitement, not your knowledge. All the knowledge that you lack right now can be given to your prospects using the weapons in T -7. Isn't that fantastic! It's all done for you. Let's face it, the weapons can explain your mission better than you can.

We've broken the skills down into two sections. **There are seven skills** that you will need to learn and in time become competent at. A few of them **you will become a Jedi Master at quite quickly, while with others you will take a bit more time to become one with the force**.

This 90-day mission is aimed to get you off the ground, and up into the atmosphere. For this to happen, **Skills 1 to 5 will be the most crucial to you**. You can earn the rank of Starship Commander using these skills over the next 90 days. If however you wish to aim for the stars, seek new planets and sunbathe on the beaches of Alpha Prime, you will need **to master Skills 6 and 7**, which we cover later. To successfully launch your ship – that is, get through the gates, onto the launch pad and lift off, **you will initially be building a customer base, getting those you know to help you. You'll also be inviting some people you know to join you for the ride.**

To successfully launch your business into the atmosphere, you'll need to become competent in the following skills:

1. Finding people

2. Inviting them to look

3. Presenting

4. Following up

5. Closing

To take your ship to the stars, you'll have to get good at the following skills:

6. Getting new recruits started

7. Promoting events

We're about to board, so let's look at how we get this ship off the launch pad. Here are the first two sets of skills that you're going to have to familiarise yourself with.

1 & 2 : FINDING PEOPLE AND INVITING THEM TO LOOK

If you're going to have initial launch success, these are the two skills that you're mostly going to be implementing to begin with.

You're already here yourself, so that's great news, because you have most likely already proven yourself to be competent, if not good, at these two basic skills. If you're new to this program and haven't yet applied them to your mission, you will have certainly, in your previous life on earth, demonstrated skills in both these areas.

We often hear some Starship Commanders jokingly say at the academy that new recruits often have to join this mission to actually be bad at it! What they mean is that you already had all the skills you need to execute a successful mission before you signed up. Don't let the fact that you have invested in this mission cause you to freeze up and stop doing what you were doing already!

Let's just explore this for one moment. You're already a natural. You've spent years on earth making friends, connecting with people, building relationships, socialising and finding people to hang out with. This is not new stuff to you. You've most likely organised some kind of event, rounded up a group of people and shared information with them.

So finding people and inviting people is not new to you. You've most likely done it time and time again, maybe without even realising it until this moment. Now you can transfer those skills to do something really special. **Being a Starship Commander isn't rocket science**. You can apply much of what you already know and the skills you have already demonstrated in your life on earth, even before this mission was an idea, right now. You're already primed for this journey. You maybe just don't know it yet!

These first two skills are known as the **gateway skills** or **launch pad skills**.

Without the ability or desire to use these skills, you can't begin to hope for a successful journey. We really do mean the gateway skills – you don't even get off the launch pad without them!

The launch pad where you're stood right now is not a place you want to stay. It's too high up, it's dangerous; you could fall off or even get frazzled by the thrusters of the other recruits talking off around you. The best place, the safest place, is on your ship. If you can to begin right now to focus most of your time and effort into developing the skills of finding and inviting people over the course of your entire journey, along with the help of your Starship Commander, you can start to reach for the stars and have everything that you want to meet your material needs: you could have an endless supply of raw material, even gold!

There's a big secret most recruits aren't aware of: if you can get good at finding and inviting, then all the other skills we're about to discuss become a whole lot easier. Sometimes you won't even need to use the other skills, because people will have already made the decision to join you. Your confidence and posture – because once you've mastered the skills you'll have a never-ending pipeline of people to speak to – will keep people attracted to you. This is a powerful position to be in. But recruits who avoid these gateways skills are often desperate in their approach. **The problem with desperation is that it alienates nearly everybody!** People aren't attracted to desperation.

Mastering the two gateways skills of connecting, listening and developing relationships, and then inviting people to join your mission means you will have a never-ending list of potential new recruits and future Starship Commanders wanting to join your mission.

This new posture you will acquire means you'll be become more confident in your role as an emerging Starship Commander and an energised leader of people. So much so that people will naturally be attracted to you and in time want to join your mission without you asking.

Make a note: in the very early stages of your mission, right now, most of your focus should go into perfecting these two skills.

3. PRESENTING

The biggest misconception about the skill of **presenting** is that you have to try and sell people on the mission. There is a reason why Starship Commanders use the expression:

Say as little as possible to as many people as possible.

The weapons outlined in T-7 are your presentations. When you previously visited weapons training, everything you needed was handed to you when it comes to presenting your mission to potential new recruits. But now we can reveal that the **last and most dangerous weapon is your own mouth**.

Your mouth is great for finding people and inviting them – but not so great when it comes to presenting. The reason you shouldn't be giving information to people by talking too much is that it's not duplicatable. What you say has a tendency to change each time depending on your emotions and it can often be unpredictable. Don't use your mouth to present the opportunity. Use the weapons provided in T-7.

How you present your mission to an individual will often depend on your relationship with and your distance from the potential new recruit.Let's recap on the presentation weapons you now have:

Mindset Before Matter

1. The Sizzler
2. The Book
3. The Room
4. The Dial-in
5. The Mentor
6. The Webinar
7. The Home

These are the weapons that you'll use to present your business to the people you know and meet. You can decide which weapon you'll use and how many times and in what order, depending on the people concerned. This we can't help you with. Just make sure you're tooled up with all the weapons before your mission begins.

Here at the academy, when we talk about inviting people we're talking about inviting them to **take a look** at something. You're inviting them to take a look at what it is you have to offer. That information is presented through the tools and weapons you have been given, as explained above.

The information about your business and your mission is presented through a video, a book, a meeting or event, or a conference call – or with the help of your support mentor and various other tools.

You may have been provided with some other tools that explain more about your mission. Ask your Starship Commander about this.

4. THE FOLLOW UP

We call this the bridging skill. This is because it **provides a bridge between success and no success, or deal / no deal**. This skill takes your prospect from somebody who has a level of interest to being either a customer or a new recruit wanting to join you on your mission. Many recruits neglect to see the importance of the follow-up and fail to spot it as one of the most important skills. But its importance is expressed by:

Fortune is in the follow-up

This should be the easiest of all the skills to master. As with others, it's a skill that you'll have used plenty of times prior to joining this mission. Up to this point, most of the hard work has already been done. You've found a person, the invite has been given, and the prospect has seen a presentation. All you have to do now is help that individual arrive at a decision to:

Take another look ...

There are two fundamental reasons why recruits fail to follow up. Perhaps more often, they are disorganised, but this may also be due to the fact that there is an expectation that the prospect is going to come running, knocking on their door, begging to join their business or to help them out as a customer. We can tell you now, though, they won't be desperate to join your mission! People don't work that way. If you've presented your opportunity correctly and there's a level of interest from your prospect, there are still a hundred things that your prospect will be prioritising above your amazing ride into space! Remember what we said earlier in the book about how we humans tend to prioritise our lists – we put the important stuff at the bottom. That includes you! So you need to follow up.

No matter how much your prospects may need you, the likelihood is that they're not going to be begging to sign up. It may happen occasionally and it's nice when it when it does – but it's not something you can rely on. So you **have to be proactive in making time with your prospect, so you can follow up with them to ascertain their level of interest.** This is why having a manageable diary is important.

Some recruits develop what's called space dementia: they can create a fantasy prospect or fantasy distributor in their head. I know we're heading for the stars and to search other galaxies – but this is the kind of fantasy you don't want.

SO WHAT IS A FANTASY PROSPECT?

This is when someone has shown a serious interest in being a customer or a new recruit and is very keen to join you and to help out on your mission. Some recruits at the academy often assume that an excited potential prospect is actually a qualified customer or distributor. But just because somebody has *agreed* to join you, that doesn't mean they have.

You still need to follow up!

This often generates a level of fear in recruits. A fear that by following up on someone, you may be pressurising them or backing them into a corner to sign, thus putting them off and sending them running a million miles away to a different side of the galaxy where you can never find them.

But a fantasy customer is no customer. A fantasy distributor is no distributor. Even if someone is super-excited to jump on board with you, this is the same as no sign-up if they have not been followed up on. You have to take the reins and follow up on everyone who sees the presentation. Ask them:

"What did you like best?"

This is a great question, because it gives you more control and usually leads to a positive outcome. It doesn't make the prospect feel like they're being backed into a corner. The purpose of the follow-up is to position yourself and the prospect for another exposure or presentation, so have your weapons ready! You can keep moving through the exposures and following up until you feel ready to close.

5. CLOSING

A good close is firstly about understanding that you're a busy person and you don't have the time to be messed around by people wasting your time. You have an incredible opportunity ... you're the one with the power, you're the future Starship Commander! **Don't give that power to your prospect** by becoming too emotionally invested in their decision.

People all over the planet **will mess you around** if you allow them to do so. This is not personal; it's what we humans do. We change our minds, prevaricate, often not realising that this can affect another individual's productivity. More importantly, *your* productivity. This is why you should always have a full pipeline of people to speak to. It makes it easier to move on if your prospect starts messing you around.

If this journey so far has taught us anything, it's that nearly all human beings love to avoid doing the tasks which are of long-term benefit. They will almost certainly, as you now know, place the **most success-driven activity** at the bottom of their list. You will have done this at some point yourself, just as we all have in the past. You may have been doing this a little bit recently, which is why you're reading this book – but that's about to change, as you're about to board your ship!

You can emotionally detach yourself from the outcome of a potential close. Don't be overly excited when someone says 'yes' to your customer proposition or your business opportunity, nor too disappointed when somebody says 'no'. Rather, try remaining neutral in both instances, as **your goal is just to get their decision, whatever it is**. Good posture here can sometime lead to a referral or sign-up further on down the line. Remember that a 'no' is only a 'no for now'. Circumstances change all the time. So don't be afraid to ask "Are you ready?"

Then celebrate *any* decision. It's the time-wasters we need to exterminate!

Getting people to make a decision, like most of the skills outlined in this chapter, won't be new to you. It's something that you've probably been doing your entire life, and this is no different in many ways.

Once you've presented people with enough information you're required to obtain a decision, and the prospect knows this.

It's important to guide your prospect to a closing answer.

People will often struggle with life-changing decisions that can improve their situation; you know this because you'll have been guilty of it too. That's why you should be so proud that you're here right now ready to take off and do something so special.

This is one of the biggest life-changing decisions you'll ever make.

Your skill with the close will be the language and the posture that you use to guide somebody to a yes/no answer:

Mindset Before Matter

1. Are you ready to get started?

2. Are you ready to do this?

3. Can we make a time to get you signed up?

4. Are you ready to give it a go?

5. Are you ready to get your order in?

6. So let's get you signed up!

The closing question must lead to action. The action is what's required, otherwise it is just your time wasted. More than any of the other skills you'll use, closing will require you to have good posture and confidence. Make sure that before you close any prospect, you have at least three other potential prospects in the pipeline. **The current appointment should never be your last appointment**. If it is, you may find it much more difficult to close your potential customer or distributor. This is because you will carry a desperate posture, which is unattractive to the prospect. **People are attracted to busy people who have lots of options**!

We have spoken about attracting people, and it's something that if you use our help you'll get better at in time. We have some great information to follow shortly after you have launched your ship. But basically, you need to make sure you're a busy person, have lots of options and speak to plenty of people.

Something people fear just as much as having to make a decision can be fear of loss. With a prospect that you feel is either procrastinating during the closing phase or avoiding commitment, here's a great tip:

Take it away from them:

"Okay, so you've seen how we can benefit you. I can see this is something you'd like to get involved in, but unfortunately at this time I'm super busy getting new people started. It's only fair that I give my time and energy to people who are ready to go *now*. So I can't continue to help you at this time, but I'm leaving the door open for you if and when you're ready to get started in the future."

This is so powerful because it does two things. First, it takes your offer away from the prospect. There is no more pressure to join, but it leaves them with a slight sense of guilt and a sense that they're an energy vampire who's wasting your precious time – which they are! But more importantly, it will allow you to have prompt closure on this particular prospect. This will alleviate any frustration in you, and remove all your need and desire to keep chasing them. You can simply move on to the next prospect who could potentially join your mission and become your next Starship Commander.

You may be presented with a situation where find you're closing a couple in a relationship. Maybe two people are buying your service or product, or joining your business. It's essential to make sure that they're both together when the decision is being made. Otherwise, despite an initial agreement from one of them, the deal is very likely to fall through.

6. GETTTING A NEW RECRUIT STARTED

If you're reading this book as a brand new recruit, the likelihood is that both your company and your Starship Commander are **helping you to get started the right way**. You may have even have been gifted this book as part of your training. Remember previous lessons. Over the next 90 days, your job is to make it to the rank of Starship Commander. That means getting your ship launched and into the atmosphere. If you can make it that far, earn your stripes and rank advance, then the next skill you're going to have to get seriously good at **is helping your new recruits get started the same way that you did.** This is key if you want to shoot for the stars and beyond.

Unlike any of the other skills covered earlier in this chapter, it's highly unlikely that you've ever had to use this skill in your life on earth – unless, that is, you've been on a similar mission in the past and you're looking to re-launch, or you're an existing Starship Commander looking for ideas.

Let's assume for now you are brand new to the program and at the beginning of your journey. Your Starship Commander may have discussed the idea of **time freedom and leverage** with you. If not, make a note in the back of this book now, and go and ask them. This concept means that one day you'll be able to set your ship onto autopilot and spend more time doing the things that you want, like visiting some other planets and moons for a holiday, upgrading your ship, and helping your friends and family back on earth. You'll be able to spend less time at the controls of your ship.

But this will only happen if you master this most important of skills to create your freedom: **getting new recruits started**.

This means you have to get good at helping your new team members take the controls, get their ships off the ground and up through the atmosphere. You have to do this with all your new recruits who join the mission until they can follow in your footsteps. Your role as you grow on this journey is to **help** those new recruits plot their own course to all becoming Starship Commanders – **but not to do the work for them!**

Getting new recruits started must be kept simple if you're to create duplication. You're going to hear a lot of talk at the academy surrounding this subject. Make sure you're in the know. It's unlikely that you'll become an expert at this before your ship leaves the atmosphere, so your Starship Commander, your mentor or whoever introduced to this mission should be helping any new recruits you bring on board to get started. This is a topic of conversation you need to have. In T -7 no 3 we talked about the role of the Mentor and how they should be helping you: this is the very first thing you need to establish once you've put this book down.

Unlike any of the other skills, it's not a skill you can afford to just be pretty good at, or your mission may become diluted in time and you won't make it to the stars. If you're fortunate enough to have a good level of support from above in the academy, then you will be sending all your new recruits to your Starship Commander to be put through the getting started program offered by your company.

Attempting to get new people started by yourself without the correct training could have a negative impact unless you're fully confident. If you currently don't have that level of support, it's important that you seek this out. You should **make a conscious effort to find support from above rather than going it alone,** otherwise there' a chance your ship will break up in the atmosphere.

Getting started is exactly what it says on the tin. It's helping a new recruit become positioned for a successful mission. **This will usually require you to assist them in bringing on their first few customers and distributors**. This process should be kept as simple as possible:

If an eight-year-old can't do it – then don't do it!

We have always found that generally **three steps** can be used to stimulate duplication on your mission, and we have found that it is very teachable to the new people boarding your ship.

Boarding the ship > Map out the controls > Launch the ship

1. Get registered.

2. Make a plan and review contact list.

3. Launch the business, as in T -5.

Essentially you need to help them action   the points in T-5. You will have to help them board the ship and get off the ground – and that's where we're taking you next. This is the only way you can ramp up your own activity, both at the beginning and for those recruits who follow you. Every recruit joining this mission should in time be able to execute these three steps. If they can't or won't, then they're not duplicating!

Similarly, if *you* aren't helping the new recruits you invite onto this mission, then *you* aren't duplicating. If this is the case, then you must refer them to your Starship Commander so that the new recruit can get started the right way. But note: if you're not prepared to do the work, it's not fair to bring people on board and hope they follow you. This is bad practice, which should be avoided. Lazy leadership is not a path you want to go down.

You will usually have 72 hours from initial registration to get the three-step Getting Started process implemented, otherwise you'll increase the chances of your new recruit failing by 80 per cent, which is unacceptable. Different social circumstances and geographical factors combined with a different work ethic mean that **no two getting started experiences will be the same**, but if you remain consistent with your getting started program, you will create distributors who will eventually duplicate.

Not everyone will duplicate to the same standard. As long as each new recruit can learn Skill 5, then you can have an amazing journey, creating long-term time freedom for yourself. **The real secret behind duplication is allowing your team to see how you do it over and over and over again**. This way it becomes a copied and a learned behaviour. You can't teach a new recruit just once how to get somebody started and then expect them to go and do it. You'll need to create a strong and family culture of participating and joining in. This all starts with you.

7. PROMOTING EVENTS

Finally before boarding, meet the **'number one wealth-building skill'** you need to develop if you wish to take your ship to the stars and beyond. Unlike the previous skills, **the problem for many when it comes to promoting is that there is no perceived value**. This is a grave error made by the vast majority of new recruits joining the program. They simply can't make the connections between promoting an event, meeting, training seminar, webinar or any other social occasion which were all highlighted in T -7. These things are designed to inspire, train and motivate you and your team. If you neglect this final skill, your journey will may before it has begun.

Similar to many of the skills highlighted in this chapter, promoting an event is not a skill which is going to be new to you. In fact, I think it would be fair to say that **promotional activity is less of a skill than it is more of a mindset.**

Consider this:

How many recruits do you think have the attitude that attending an event will **cost them money or time that they don't have?**

If you're a poor promoter, and don't attend events yourself, the feelings, attitudes and behaviours you have towards this particular skill will be passed down to the team members you bring along for the ride. Essentially **what you will end up with is a team of people who neither attend nor promote the events for the company they invested in in the first place**.

Back on Planet Earth, think about would happen if you never attended any of the meetings, trainings or events run by your place of employment. Do you think you'd ever be promoted? Do you think you'd progress? Do you think that you might even lose your job? We can't kick you out of this program for not attending or promoting events. We don't need to, because if you don't you'll fail and leave all by yourself.

Humans beings have never understand the notion of investing in themselves, **purely because it's not a learned behaviour that you**

acquired before joining this mission. Back on earth you'll have been taught to invest in shares, artwork, jewellery or a vintage car, maybe even a nice watch, because of all those things are expected to go up in value over time – but never a voyage in a spaceship.

But what **if *you* want to go up in value?** You yourself are an asset, and the biggest one you'll ever have. This means you have to invest in yourself. You may have to invest a bit time and money in yourself instead of allowing your current social diet to command your value.

This means investing in personal development and self-education. Over time, developing your knowledge and understanding of your business and your mission, acquiring the right mindset and associating with like-minded people. **You can only acquire these things by joining in and participating with the positive associations you obtain from these events**. It really is that simple. **Your existing environment isn't working for you: if it was you wouldn't be here.**

If you're going to be successful , you must mimic the behaviour of the successful people at the academy. You can't simply keep doing what you've always done. We learned that lesson in T -9. You can't continue with the same habits and make the same choices you've always made. If you do, you'll always remain the same – and now that you've got this far, I don't believe that you want that.

Over the next 90 days, you need to try and attend as many events as possible. You should be proactive in this and have your diary or calendar filled with everything that's taking place. Make filling your diary a job tonight! Note the events down at the back of this book!

You need to position yourself in this business to become somebody who's known to your network and your peers. This will give you a sense of belonging and family, which will encourage you to stick with the business through difficult times. It will also provide you with the positive association you need, which will become addictive – and more importantly it will inspire and encourage you to bring all your new recruits and team members along. It's not a popularity contest, and it's important not to attend events just to be seen. Rather, have a strategy for helping people get to know your face – and of course, most importantly, to know your story.

Events are a great way to help you get to the front of the room. This may appear daunting now, but in the future it will be hugely beneficial to you. Its not mandatory – you dont have to become a speaker – important for your team to eventually see you as a person of influence.

Let go of your ego. We see it time and time again – recruits getting carried away with their own glory. But until you reach the stars, you'll be promoting other peoples events. You're not the star of the show yet. You're not the bride in the wedding, nor the corpse in the funeral. Back on earth, if you've organised birthdays, weddings and other events that centre around you, there is clear proof that you have the skills and ability to promote. Now you can be rewarded for promoting and elevating other people until the time comes for you to shine, if thats what you want.

Every Starship Commander should make it clear that you dont actually get paid for introducing new recruits. You get paid when those new recruits start to perform. They won't start to perform unless theyre joining in and participating in company events – and that includes you! It's simple science, its physics, and neither you nor any bending of the space-time continuum can change this rule. Many have tried!

It doesn't matter whether it's a company convention held once a year, a local team meeting, a team seminar, a social media webinar or a dial-in conference call. These are all the events which are designed to plug your new recruits into this mission and be a catalyst for success. Promoting an event requires you to reach out to people and explain to them:

1. Why they need to be there.
2. Who's going to be speaking.
3. How they can go about booking.

Good and bad habits start from the top: they start with *you*. We trust that you've understood most of the information provided in Skills School. Please feel free to go back and make some notes and revisit this information. Extract the basics you need: the rest you can learn later, as we're now about to board!

T -5

WELCOME ON BOARD

Welcome on board! Isn't she beautiful? You finally made it this far. Congratulations! Let us show you around the cockpit and the control panels. Get familiar with it all and buckle up, then we can be on our way. This is where the fun begins ...

The information you've received in the first half of this book should serve you well as we move forward into the second half, which is where the real work begins. We hope you like the inside of your ship; you're going to be here for a while.

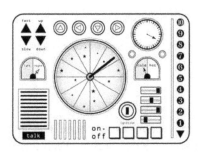

This is so cool; you're celebrating something huge here: the launch of your business, and your mission to venture where few people will ever go in their lifetime! Doesn't that make you feel great? Like you're progressing and getting better with every word you read!

Stepping inside for the first time can be daunting, but you need to remain focused. The last thing we want is to stall and have a failure to launch situation – not now, when you've already made it further than most. If this ship can't get enough thrust early on, then it'll struggle to get off the ground. You could say that this is the most important part of the entire journey. Right here and right now is where we see most of the setbacks occur. Furthermore, if we can't gather enough momentum in the next 72 hours since you boarded this ship, this can have a negative effect over the entire next 90-day launch period. But neither of these things needs to happen now, though – not after your training

When you successfully make it to Starship Commander, this is something you will need to bear in mind when helping your new recruits launch their ships. This is something you'll be faced with. This is why the Getting Started process is so important

So take a good look at the controls; make sure you're familiar with most of them. You don't need to know it all: just remembering a few things and doing them well is enough to get you out there.

LAUNCHING

Only a sense of progress will ensure that you want to carry on and not turn back when the going gets tough. Good launches always start off with a mass explosion in the first 72 hours.

Here at the academy, we call this:

(A condensed burst of activity)

Back on earth, you may have experienced this in the form of inviting people to an event, party or a celebration. With any real celebration, you must make sure that invitations are all sent out at the same time. This is because all the positive responses you will get will help your body to produce dopamine. Dopamine is a neurotransmitter that helps control the brain's reward and pleasure centres. Dopamine also helps regulate movement and emotional responses, and it enables us not only to see rewards, but also to take action to move toward them. Taking action is fundamental to your launch.

Some recruits join this program only to treat it like a death sentence. **You should be more excited than anybody when it comes to your mission**. You should be as high as a kite!

But if you're not, then you need to examine the reasons why you're feeling this way: go back to T -9 and T -8 and see if you can find the answer.

Stepping inside this ship for the first time can often create a misconception that **inviting lots of people to join or help you is scary**. You will hear the word 'fear' being thrown around a lot by some of the recruits at the academy. This is a hugely misguided notion and a self-fulfilling prophecy; in fact, this exercise is a much simpler one than you may have initially thought or than people would have you believe.

I'm glad we've cleared that up. Now if we can move on ...

EVERYTHING STARTS WITH AN INVITATION

You've been inviting people to all manner of things for light-years. So inviting people is not a new idea or concept, nor should it be treated as such. We touched on this in Skills School. For this journey, there are three key things you need to know before you **make your first 30 invitations to those people on your list to join on this mission as a team member or help your mission along by becoming a valued customer:**

1. Invite people at the same time

2. Know what you're inviting them to look at

3. Be excited / tell them why / ask for help.

The beauty of making an invite is that we exist in a time and a space where you can quickly and effectively invite multiple people to a single event to explore a single idea while following the crucial principle to make all those invites individual, targeted to the specific person.

No recipient of an invite to anything wants to feel like they're part of a group, not important enough that you couldn't reach out to them individually. People need to feel special. **That means acknowledging them by name and preferably letting them hear your voice.**

There are many ways to invite people along for this ride, but the main thing is allow them to hear the **excitement and urgency** and the **passion in your voice**. This simply can't be replaced by any other form of communication. Too many recruits attempt to make invitations the lazy way, using what we call a shotgun approach. Blasting out a single invite hoping 30 people will bite – it simply doesn't work that way. If you did that all you'd do would be to injure lots of people and yourself in the process. Not cool!

When you're about to take off, you must hand in your **checklist of potential recruits**. Your Starship Commander will refer to this as your **contacts list**. This is a written list of around 100 people **who you'd be happy to invite to your wedding day**. We ask you to do it this way so that you don't prejudice those people who you decide wouldn't be appropriate for this mission. If you **don't** have that list already, you need to add this job to your priority list at the back of this book.

CONTACTS LIST

Don't hand your Starship Commander a small piece of scrap paper with a handful of names on it. This is about your attitude to the whole mission, so make sure you have a list in a spreadsheet on a flash drive, or neatly written in a journal, notebook or the back of this book. Ensure that there is a certain level of chronology, starting with those closest to you or, as we say, the 'hottest'. These are the people who you'd approach in either an emergency or if you were excited about something, just like this mission. You should be excited about that!

At the back of this book, we have provided a space for you to write first 30 contacts you will be approaching as part of this launch process. But there may be certain geographical or social factors that **could affect the way they use your service product or join your business**. Where are they located on the planet? Make sure you have a note of this on your list. It will also affect your presentation method. Refer to the basic weapons in T -7 for those.

You may have a particularly negative or unsupportive person on your list. It's still important to include such a name on the list because if you're struggling with adding 30 names this one may give you a trigger to recall some other people you may know or may have met. You don't have to actually contact people you don't like, but they could be useful to you in moving forward. You may also find some nice surprises from people who respond more positively than you had imagined at first. Try to avoid any prejudging.

THIS MISSION IS TO INVITE 30 CONTACTS

Now your thrusters are fired up, you should have this plan mapped out.

It's likely that exposing this many people to your business will help you in your quest to introduce **your first 10 valued customers** and your **first 3 to 5 new team members**. This will only happen if you use the skills listed in T -6 in the correct way. Skills 1–5 will be the most important initially, and you should have your Starship Commander on standby to help you with Skill 6, to help get your recruits started. Then you'll need to use Skill 7 to promote events to your new recruits.

One of the things you want to avoid, now that your ship's moving in an upward direction, is a certain reaction you may get from people you know. At the end of the day, you're on a ship heading for the stars, so of course they're going to ask questions. **The number one question** from people that often throws new recruits is:

"What are you doing that for? You're not a salesperson!"

This question can take you down a negative road which is difficult to pull back from. You want to avoid any question like this, and there's an easy fix. You just have to be prepared! It's always important to promote rather than defend. That means you need to either praise any questions from people –

"Hey, I'm glad you asked that question!" –

or – much better – prevent the question from being asked in the first place.

How? With your initial invite, **you share a very brief story or give a reason why you're doing this**. Even if your reason may be embarrassing, the truth sets you free! Be open and transparent about why you're on this mission, irrespective of how worried you are about your current social or financial situation. Being excited and giving the people you contact a reason why you're embarking on this journey will in most cases trigger an **emotional understanding and connection** between you and your friend or relative. Then they won't even feel the need to ask!

The third and final part of the invite is the magic word that every new recruit should learn in their first 90 days. It's a word you should be using more than any other:

HELP !

People would rather help you than be helped by you. The appeal for 'Help!' is one of the most understated treasures of the human language. We often fail to realise its true potential and power. We don't understand that **help is one of the things that another human being will rarely refuse to another** when asked directly and individually. Asking for help from your nearest and dearest is your key language tool during this important phase, as your ship is taking off.

Your mission is to invite 30 people over the next 90 days to look at what you're doing. You may have been issued some scripts by your Starship Commander. These can be useful guides if you're not 100 per cent confident about knowing what to say to people on your contacts list. The only thing to be aware of with the scripts is that they can often remove the human element from your personality. This is something that your nearest and dearest may sense if you're not behaving as yourself during this time. So it's always best to be yourself, be authentic and use the simple invitation guidelines in this book.

If, now you're on this mission, you become somebody different this can arouse suspicion from your closest friends and family. So if you're not careful, this can sometimes backfire on you. Be yourself! That's what they want to see in you.

THE MAGIC FIVE RULE

The **magic five rule** is pretty fantastic, and can help you get your business off the ground quickly and really boost this launch process. Some recruits fail to program it into their control systems because they haven't been taught it prior to launch. *But here it is for you.*

The magic five rule means that there will be five people who you could ask to be your first customer/helper, or at least to try your services and products, to help get your ship off the ground.

Those five people will also have a magic five, so acquiring your first 25 helpers could happen quickly if you're smart. Using this method will massively fuel those thrusters on your ship.

During the acquisition of your first few recruits and customers, it's important not to give them any information during the invite process. **The benefits of your product or service will be explained in the presentation steps. Your weapons will handle this.** Your first step to success is to share your story and explain to people why you're on this mission. You can then suggest to them that it would be a big help if they look at what you're doing.

We hope you're enjoying the ride so far. Look out the window and see how far you've come! It's time to step it up a gear shift.

People make decisions based on emotion, not data. So use **emotion for the invitation** and **information for the presentation**: not the other way round. This style of invitation will alleviate any feeling in yourself that you're a salesperson. This feeling is something that many recruits signing up to this journey fear most. But if you apply this method you won't have this fear. There's a lot of talk about fear at the academy in new recruits. Sadly this is a self-fulfilling prophecy. But in fact, fear is never the issue. **It's preservation of self-image, looking stupid and people asking you, "What are you doing *that* for?"**

If you want to remove any sense of stupidity or sales-style tactics in yourself, asking for help is your best way forward. You will be positioned to expose people to this incredible opportunity and get a sense of whether it may be a fit for them.

Now you have lift-off, take some time to sit down with your Starship Commander or whoever introduced you, map out a route and make the invites together. This is because if you're not accountable to somebody there's a good chance that you won't do it. This is common error that most people make when starting out. This is your business, and we don't want you stalling so early on in the mission.

AN EFFECTIVE WAY TO COMMUNICATE

People don't generally pick up the phone as they once did, and they can often miss a voicemail you leave. Sometimes you don't even know if they've heard your message. This can be a frustrating problem if you want to move at speed early on. We're not discounting this form of communication – phone calls and speaking to people will play a huge role in your business – but we also need to be mindful of how human behaviour has changed.

THE VOICE MEMO

We've equipped your ship with a very clever intercom system. **The power of the voice memo is becoming widely used** by many Starship Commanders and their new recruits.

You will be familiar with services such as:

- WhatsApp
- Facebook
- Messenger

and various other systems that allow you at the touch of a finger to send a pre-recorded voice message to your friends, family and other people you know. The power of a voice memo is huge. Let us explain why. It's almost guaranteed to be seen and heard by the person you're inviting, as it works the same as an instant message. You have the added bonus of knowing that they have listened to or seen it. The most powerful aspect, and why it's our favourite, is that they **get to hear your voice,** which is important as this is an emotional exercise.

You can also use text and phone-based invitations, as some people may not use a voice memo system – but consider, when you put this all together, what you have with a voice memo is an instant voicemail which makes the emotional connection with an individual thus minimising the likelihood of objection or resistance. Finally, the message always gets through!

You can easily work this part of the mission in a condensed burst, as we previously discussed. Right now as your ship is headed up, you should be prepping this.

If you invite people via voice memo or message, please bear in mind that messages will all arrive at different points in time.

Please take this into account, and consider how people's busy lifestyle and how they prioritise their daily routines will determine how quickly they reply to you. You have been prepped for this earlier. Relax: not everyone is going to rush to get back to you and help you at the same time, so be prepared for this. Even those closest to you won't necessarily have you down as their number one priority. Have your expectations firmly set out! It's your job to manage your responses from people, not the other way around.

YOUR LOOKING FOR A POSITIVE RESPONSE

There is never an exact science as to how your first 30 people will respond to your invitation. What I will say, though, from observing past recruits, is that what you are looking for first is a positive response from the people that you know, resulting in the dopamine fix that gets you going. Their response will be partly down to your invitation, which you know how to do now. Depending on the individual, their geography and their social circumstances, this will then determine which of the weapons you will use to present your business. Take a moment to revisit T -7 to see how you can make a presentation to someone who's responded positively.

It's important to note that **the positive response** is really all that you should be looking for initially. If you can attract these, then you will lessen the chances of stalling your ship.

HANDLING UNEXPECTED RESPONSES

The number one question asked by recruits at the academy is: How do you deal with negative-minded friends and family? As humans we prejudge – it's in our DNA – and we are also massively emotionally attached to our expectations of how people should treat us and respond to us. If those expectations are not met, this can throw you off course, bouncing you off your trajectory. You'll almost certainly encounter an unexpected or unwelcome response from somebody you know – and it may even be from somebody closest to you. An alien attack is how we like to refer to it.

This can sting sometimes; after all, you're excited about your mission and becoming a Starship Commander, and to have that excitement undermined by somebody you care about can hurt. All we can say is that the correct form of invitation will minimise this. Doing it your way will almost certainly hurt you, but doing it the way we teach you won't: **follow us, and you should never have to handle negativity**.

Love them, but don't let their opinions decide your fate!

Accept that if you make it to Starship Commander in time they will warm to you, and some may even join you. It's not about you: you have to earn respect – it's not an entitlement.

BUT I THOUGHT YOU WERE MY FRIEND

The role of a friend is to engage with you socially and help you on occasion if required. But it doesn't entitle you to expect that they should fully support, accept and follow your path and be happy for you at the same time. The fact is that many people would rather see somebody other than their friend score big. You may be different, but your first path to success is to have a firm grip on human behaviour and how people make decisions and why they make the decisions that they do.

You're very lucky to be here; only a tiny percentage of people get to ride this journey. Many people will never be given the opportunity to change their lives – and even if they are, most people are not built to seize it: for many, opportunity is an obstacle in the road, and one to be avoided. Despite this, you live in the best time for this kind of journey; more people than ever are open to new ideas than ever there have been. This brave new world and this new economy have forced people on earth to open their eyes to other things. More and more young people are plugging into the idea that one revenue stream is not enough, and that the path to enlightenment is through personal development and self-education.

You are special. Right now you're in the lucky 3 per cent who've been offered a chance to leave this planet. More importantly, you have the power to help others and to empower them with the gift of choice.

That's your mission over the next 90 days. It's time to get a grip on these controls and take this ship into the clouds.

T -4

LEAVING HOME

Congratulations! You've sky rocketed past the halfway mark, but you can't get this ship into the atmosphere and beyond unless you're willing to leave your home-based mindset. Your worldly goods, your precious belongings and the home you built – none of these things are going anywhere. The only thing that has to move right now is *you*!

Your surroundings and environment will start to change as time speeds up and you move closer to the stars. There will also be some things that won't move and many things that stay the same. What kind of changes do you expect to happen, and what changes do you want to happen? These are things you need to give consideration to. Note them down at the back of this book now.

FIRST RULE OF CHANGE

You can't change the people around you, **but you can change your environment**, and you can become a better person and have a greater influence on those **who truly need** you. Remember, the difference between somebody not needing you and needing you may just be a matter of weeks or months, not the words that you speak. You can't get people to need your help!

In time the people you meet, the friends that you make, the conversations that you have, the possessions that you own and the thoughts and feelings that you have will grow and change for the better as your journey on this mission continues, **as you glide up the success curve in your ship.**

You will encounter new species, new people and new life forms, and you will make new connections and visit places you never knew existed. People **you don't even know right at this moment** ,whose life you will touch in the not too distant future, are out there in the galaxy, waiting for you to come and take them away for a life less ordinary.

People who may have turned their back on you before, people who were not there to help you at the beginning – many of these people will one day reach out to you for help when they're ready and positioned to make that choice, just as you once did. It's your job to come back for them when they're ready to talk. They say home is where the heart is, but the greatest things you will experience, some of the biggest moments of accomplishment and the largest tracks you lay down for your success will happen **when you're away from your home**.

Many of the people your care about **won't grow and change** with you, but most will always be there for you in their own way. Accept that some may not understand your journey, many will not want to hear about it, others will be afraid that every time you return home to see them you will be there as a reminder to them of what they are not doing but perhaps should be. The important thing to remember is to understand and accept that you must and fly and let live.

YOUR HOME IS YOUR FORTRESS

The four walls that protect you from the outside world are designed to keep you safe. This is the notion you will need to let go of now if you're to get through the atmosphere. Over the next 90 days and beyond into your mission, you need to be leaving your home as much as you possibly can.

Every opportunity you get to get out should be done with the realisation that **the walls that keep you safe can sometimes be the walls that lead to your ultimate failure and lack of progress**. There is no success in safety and shelter!

YOU'RE PART OF AN INCREDIBLE FORCE

You're part of a brotherhood and sisterhood of people who think differently. There's nothing like being part of a small group of people who have their eyes wide open. There's nothing wrong with being in a minority. That's why you should treat your home as the walls that may sometimes be holding you back, rather than believing it 's a refuge keeping you safe. Your ship will safely transport you to events, trainings, seminars and business socials, giving you the chance to mix and associate with other recruits like you. It will take you to appointments to see potential customers and distributors and to meet with new team members and those hoping to join you. These are all opportunities to leave your four walls and to grow into the Starship Commander we know you will one day be. Every time that front door closes behind you takes you one step closer towards your ultimate goal.

YOUR HOME IS YOUR COMMAND CENTER

It's your mission control, where many of the foundations to your journey will be laid. It should be used as a central location to hold meetings with your recruits. You can engage in personal development and self-education in your home, and even attend the online webinars and other online social training events we discussed earlier from the comfort of your own home.

It's from your home that you can operate your DMO (daily method of operation). Our first book, *Mindset Before Matter – for your Network Marketing Journey*, showed how to use an effective daily method of operation. If you haven't read it we suggest you get hold of a copy from Knowledge is King or Amazon. We would also appreciate your review of this material on Amazon after you've read it: just search on *Mindset Before Matter*. Amazon and Knowledge is King are two hugely useful resources for sourcing further education.

In your previous life, your survival was largely down to your actions and instincts when outside the home. In the early part of the 21st century, we saw the introduction of social media, which I'm sure you will be very familiar with and use frequently. Of course, platforms such as Facebook, Instagram, Pinterest and Snap Chat, and technology such as WhatsApp and instant messaging have caused an incredible cultural shift over the last decade, and these are all massively powerful tools to assist in the growth of your business. But at the time of writing only a small per cent of recruits use these tools to positive effect, so it's worth speaking to your mentor about learning how to get better at using social media to the benefit of your business.

With the increased dependency on the internet –online shopping, online gambling and the power of cinema being brought to your living room amongst other things – this wave of cultural change is causing people to stay at home and to socialise less. The loss of ability to form lasting relationships, the weakened conversation skills, the loss of language can generate greater insecurity and anxiety amongst young people and some older people, arousing questions of self-worth and feelings of inadequacy through the daily practice of comparing our lives to those of others. We can wake up to a diet of scrolling through the lives of others and hypnotising ourselves into believing we're not good enough.

Much of this has been brought on because we're leaving our home less. So you can help create a cultural shift that gets people out more into the fresh air, into an environment that promotes growth and communication. Move away from the Hollywood celebrity lifestyle that creates insecurity at the top and inadequacy at the bottom.

Your work will come home with you, and if you've joined this journey not just for you but also because of those that you love, they will need to accept that. The people around you need to be more accepting of your individuality. But choose caution. **People are often less concerned with what's in your best interest and more concerned with their emotional responses to your actions**. Your home is the box where you eat, sleep and spend time with the family. **You will need to adapt and make room to facilitate your command centre.**

Have boundaries where you can separate the two, and then where and when you can, include the people that you love in what you're doing. When the time comes for you to go out, whether it's for an event, appointment or training, you may need to remind them of why you're on this mission. Your home and the people in it need to be a part of the solution and part of your journey. It's your responsibility to try and facilitate this. **Many problems in the home can be solved before they start by including the people around you in your mission.**

If you want people to take you seriously, show them that you're serious about the actions that you take. A strong home relies on two elements: first, strong foundations, which are created through your team; and second, life, people inside, having conversations in an environment filled with the energy of heat and light. These are your customers. Neither of these can survive without the other.

Your home at times will not want you to leave. It will put up resistance, mentally and socially and you need to be ready when it does.

T -3

ALIENS AND ASTEROIDS

Watch out up here! There are some things up ahead you need to mindful of. Aliens and asteroids can be obstacles that you'll face during your mission and on your onward journey. They can be manifested in number of different forms. Fortunately for you, you've been well trained and taught how to access the weapons and skills you need in order to handle most of what you're approaching.

On your mission, you will find that **aliens usually only attack when you've provoked them or have approached them incorrectly.** Should you misuse the skills laid down in this book, you could increase the risk of unwanted reactions from those around you in respect of your mission. This can send you way off course. Some aliens may even attempt to sabotage your mission if you go on the offensive without due care.

At this point all those who are closest to you **should be treated with the utmost care,** as they can often display alien behaviour that you didn't see coming. This can cause a collision course if you are not mentally prepared.

You will encounter three species of alien on your journey:

- Hot-blooded
- Warm-blooded
- Cold-blooded

HOT BLOODED ALIENS

Hot-blooded aliens are by far the most dangerous on this mission, and if you're not careful they can often be the cause of early mission failure. You will usually have an emotional connection with this species. They know you, they know your story, they know what you're about, and they understand where you've been before. This can put you at a disadvantage, because they tend to judge you more than any of the other aliens and will often be the most oppressive if you're not careful. They will slow down your progress early on if you don't approach them the right way, as specified in this book.

73

Hot-blooded aliens will be the first type that you encounter on your mission. In fact, as you've made it this far you will most likely have already encountered them. For all their downsides, **they care about you more than any other species**, so you'll need to approach them from an emotional perspective so that you don't find yourself on the defensive. Both offending and defending can and should be avoided at all costs.

They will be willing to help you – but it's your responsibility and your duty to treat them the right way. Hot-blooded aliens can sting you the most if you get a negative reaction during your mission. It's important for you to remain excited and urgent at all times with your goals of the mission, as specified in T -5.

They are **not interested in your help**, and sometimes if you don't use a considered approach you can arouse **suspicion about your motives**.

KNOWING YOUR "WHY" IS KEY

A huge line of defence in avoiding any alien attack, particularly from the hot-blooded species, is by firstly explaining to them why you're embarking on this mission and asking for their help, as we explained when you boarded. This is by far the best way to neutralise and forestall the sometimes unenthusiastic nature of this species.

Alien attacks are easily avoidable, despite the stories you may hear from various Starship Commanders. You can have fun with this species as long as you remember that the aliens are not the problem. **Remember that you cannot control their response or reaction to you**. What you *can* control, though, is how you approach them and how you treat them and interact with them.

An effective invite executed with consideration for who you're speaking to will usually give the outcome you desire. First and foremost you need to get a positive response from this group of people; we touched on this in earlier chapters. You know what to do! You may hear some Starship Commanders speak of how some of their newer recruits have suffered attacks by hot-blooded aliens, trash talking about how unsupportive they are and how they can throw recruits off track with their negative behaviour towards our mission. Personally, we believe that if you've understood the lessons in this book and if you familiarise yourself with how to correctly treat this particular species, then you should be able to keep all most negative, uninvited and unwanted responses to an absolute minimum.

There is no question that our relationship with the hot-blooded aliens is a far more strained relationship than with any other species. You have to appreciate the emotional and often volatile nature of the relationship you have with them. Respect the fact that hot-blooded aliens care about you. Their response to you and your mission is usually going to be **born out of emotion and not logic**. Your notion of how they should be behaving and reacting towards you will often **be met with an unexpected outcome**. The fact is, you don't know who will react positively and who will react negatively. You don't know who will join you, who will help you on your journey and who will ignore you, perhaps even respond negatively towards you. You may even have some nice surprises. You now have the power, the skills and the weapons to remain consistent when dealing with them.

These aliens are hypersensitive, and aware of any changes in your behaviour. If you start speaking to them and behaving in a different way from normal, you will arouse suspicion. If you do this, they're likely to be less cooperative.

This is because they're often unable to differentiate between you, their friend, relative or loved one and the fact that you could be a potential Starship Commander. They simply can't get their head around this. It is for this very reason that you should approach them with the full knowledge **of why you have decided to embark on this mission**. Explaining why you are doing this will allow them to connect emotionally with the idea of what you're doing. This can then position you for a conversation with them.

Hot-blooded aliens will ultimately be responsible for helping you smash through your first 90 days and get this ship through the clouds. **Treat them with the respect they deserve** and follow the guidance we have given you.

WARM BLOODED ALIENS

Far less dangerous than hot-blooded, mainly because you're **less likely to be concerned about how they react to you**. While they will generally be less inclined to help you straight away, you have the power to create a strong connection with them by reconnecting with them and showing a sincere interest in them. We suggest that with this species that you reach out and reconnect with them to find out what has been going on in *their* life. With this species, the first objective is to **re-establish or strengthen an existing relationship**, something you don't need to do with the hot- blooded alien.

While this means a little more effort on your part, they're far less likely to prejudge you. With warm-blooded aliens, you will most likely have the widest relationship range.

They could be either:

- a good friend who you have *not spoken to in a while,* or
- someone you don't know that well but have *interacted with recently.*

Whichever sort, they will need to be handled with care. You will need to be more genuinely interested in them for their own sake than in getting them to help you or make a sale. If you adopt this strategy correctly, you will be **positioned to reconnect** in such a way that you will in time be able to ask for help or share your idea with them and invite them to look.

If this is somebody who you've spoken to recently but **you are not particularly close to** such as:

- somebody who you met at a party, or
- somebody who did work for you or provided a service, or
- a friend of a friend,

then you can use your skill of connecting by placing **value on their feedback** and **their opinion**, as opposed to selling your story immediately.

Warm-blooded aliens who you don't have a pre-existing relationship with are usually less interested in your story unless they happen to be a very 'interested' person – in which case, great! – but you don't get too many of these. If they do show an interest in you, then it'll be easy to get them to look in response to your invitation.

This type of alien, who you're less familiar with, will often respond positively if you can feed their ego and position them as a person of importance in your life. Remember, your task is to get them to look, no more. Think back to what we said about the feeling of reward and 'action. You can produce dopamine, the happy drug, in people by making them feel special. (You may want to note this down here. When you write something down, it helps carve it into the brain.) This warm-blooded species will be important to you. Especially if for whatever reason you have alienated or burned out all the hot-blooded aliens.

Understanding why your relationship with this particular species is warm is very important. Is this somebody you know? If so, how well do you know them, and how long has it been since you last spoke with them? You should be reconnecting with the person **void of motive**, and with the sole purpose of finding out **how _they_ are** and **what _they_ have been up to.** This will undoubtedly produce a more positive result than simply reconnecting with them to try and **sell them on _your_ journey**. That will most likely not work for you. This is one of the biggest mistakes that recruits make on this mission. Place yourself in the position of this species. How would you feel if someone **you had not seen in a while reached out to you** with the obvious intention of either trying to sell you something or getting you to enrol in something or with some other motive to benefit them, not you?

Every species of alien wants to feel special; they want to have a voice. No one wants to feel like they are part of a list you're ploughing through – even though in essence that is what you may be doing. All three species are very clever **and will sense intent and motive** if it's not appropriate and if you're not careful. Treat people on an individual basis and show that you care about them. Be a better listener than you are a speaker.

Your greatest assets are your ears, not your mouth.

If you have the ability to listen and be genuinely interested in other species, this forestalls the hostility that we hear some recruits complain about. You are ultimately responsible for people's reactions towards you. They can be controlled if you listen, care and connect. Kill the motive!

COLD BLOODED ALIENS

The most misunderstood of all three species. For so many years our number one error is that we have mistreated and misnamed cold-blooded aliens.

There is **no such thing** as a cold-blooded alien …

While we are on our mission, we may forget one thing: **as soon we begin to interact** *with this particular species* **they become warm**.

For training purposes, it has always been deemed easier to refer to them as cold because we don't know them – and that is precisely the problem. The problem with the word 'cold' is that it suggests they were not expecting you and that you arrived unannounced to drag them onto your ship. In the past some recruits have treated them as cold, arriving unnoticed without permission or invitation. This nearly always backfires. You *must not* do this!

Some recruits have been caught blasting out unsolicited links and messages to people they don't know or have had no previous relationship with – firing off their weapons in all directions before they even know the names. Some recruits have done this unknowingly, some have just had poor training and some are just damn lazy! It doesn't work. If you behave in this way, you could end up being kicked off the Starship Commander program and might even damage the academy's reputation. Our program gets a bad rap, not because it's dangerous but because of the behaviour of certain recruits. You need to be an ambassador for the Starship Commander program and not tarnish its reputation with poor practice.

If you want to survive encounters with the cold-blooded alien …

… there must be a certain level of engagement between you and this species before any invitation can be made. One of the hardest yet most important things for any recruit to do to sustain the longevity of their journey is to **transform cold-blooded aliens into hot or warm-blooded aliens**. This is perhaps the number one thing all recruits struggle with.

'Finding people' in T -6 relates to this. You find people by connecting with them and adding them to your list. Would it help if we just said, 'Make a friend' – ?

Some recruits struggle to make friends – not because they can't, but because they've forgotten the art of making friends, building relationships and making connections; they believe they **can't enter into a**

conversation without motive. So lose the motive and you'll make friends. Harnessing this power will surely be a catalyst to help you reach for the stars and hit the rank of Starship Commander.

You need to be most respectful of cold-blooded aliens, because right now they are the vast majority of the population. They are the many when it comes to your future team, your future customers and your future friends. You just don't know it yet. That's why having vision is so very important. Every idea you execute should consider the future. Quick fixes and instant gratification are part of the average mindset, which focuses on survival. But these are not the characteristics of a Starship Commander. Cold-blooded aliens are 100 million to one by comparison with all the other types of alien. While hot-blooded aliens are your focus right now through your first 90-day mission, much of your long-term success will rely on building your relationships with cold-blooded aliens.

Transform cold-blooded aliens into hot-blooded aliens – not cold-blooded aliens into enemies that slate our profession as Starship Commanders. What you do should be about conversation, not conversion.

Cold-blooded aliens are everywhere. They're powerful and they have a voice. They could do you and us harm if you're not part of the solution. They have no emotional attachment to our program or to you, and unlike hot-blooded aliens they will respect you more as an expert in your field if you do this correctly. They will be less inclined to prejudge you on where you've been previously and where you are now. They can process data far more rapidly than hot-blooded aliens. Even more so than warm-blooded aliens. Not because they have higher intelligence, but because they have a low emotional investment in you. Cold-blooded aliens can have all the strengths and none of the weaknesses of hot and warm-blooded aliens. If you can warm them up, they'll listen to you void of emotion and judgment. The future of this mission will ultimately rest on your ability to turn cold-blooded aliens into warm and hot ones, so do not try to recruit any into your program until you've given yourself a chance to get to know them.

ASTEROIDS

These are pesky little things and they can be a common occurrence on this mission, but nothing that you won't be able to figure out or get help with. They're something you'll learn to handle as you advance to Starship

Commander. Get used to them, because the further your journey progresses, the more asteroids are going to collide with your ship. The problem with asteroids is that they're far less predictable than aliens, and you have less control over where and when they may strike.

They can take different forms and can appear when you least expect them: you have to expect ups and downs on the upward curve of success. Some collisions are only small and will make tiny dents in your ship, while some much larger asteroids can do significantly more damage, changing your trajectory and sending you off course until you recover.

Some asteroids are simply cosmetic, so while the good looks of your ship may be compromised, everything still functions just fine. Other asteroids can damage your control system. Becoming aware of the difference between **your ego being the issue** and **there being a real technical difficulty** is very important in getting a problem fixed. Understanding the nature of asteroids is key – differentiating between those that cause cosmetic problems and those that cause mechanical ones. On any journey to self-improvement, while you're striving for success you will have setbacks.

It's fair to say, too, that if you're not having to deal with aliens and asteroids **your journey is headed in the wrong direction**. Most likely, your ship is still on the launch pad – or even worse, heading for a black hole. What we're saying here is that you need to see these problems for what they really are – a good thing, because they're keeping you on the success curve. Try to dispel any notions that avoiding problems and keeping safe is a good thing on this mission. You will have been taught in your previous life to avoid danger – but it's important to be able to differentiate between rational dangers like death and what your body is **telling you to avoid because it makes you feel uncomfortable; this is something you can and should work through, because it will**

make you stronger. If the need is great enough you will discover this quickly.

Cosmetic problems caused by an asteroid have a general tendency to arise when people don't see things the way you do. Some people will disagree with you. They may do and say things in a negative way that you hadn't expected. At this point, your ego and pride may take a knock, but it's important to note that whatever cosmetic problems arise in your first 90 days – and certainly when moving forward on your journey – it will have very little, if any, bearing on the overall success of your mission. If your customers cancel or a team member quits the journey, you can't afford to make yourself the issue. Cosmetic damage caused by smaller asteroids such as these are the most frequent. They will happen, so get ready – but they really are harmless, so wire your brain to accept that these things are simply part of your warp trail. They'll stick around behind you for a while and then eventually disappear. As you're getting closer to hitting the rank of Starship Commander, you'll be faced with this more often, but the rewards of your mission will in turn become greater.

As your responsibility and your skills grow, other people will rely on you to lead, to become a troubleshooter and a problem solver. It's not uncommon for this to happen in your first 90 days, so don't feel handicapped by your brief time spent on this mission so far. If you're a novice on this journey, you still have a lifetime of experience when it comes to survival on earth. Early on in this book, we explained that you shouldn't discount what you've previously learned and experienced. While what you learned before joining this mission isn't essential to your overall success, you may be able to draw on your past experience to help you in sticky situations. After all, you've survived on earth until now.

You've been through a lot. What you've dealt with on earth over the last few decades should give you the strength to push through. If you've survived the last 20 years on earth, you can survive the next 90 days blasting through the atmosphere.

A situation you will likely encounter at some point is an asteroid field. Although these are infrequent, they can create enough damage to send you crashing back to earth.

Here they come …

Mindset Before Matter

An asteroid field is a particular nuisance because it makes dents in your ship and can affect your control systems at the same time. Such a sequence of events can create tensions between you and those you've brought on the mission, and they can cause logistical and mechanical problems when it comes to the process. When things aren't going your way and the world seems against you, **you're probably experiencing an asteroid field**. The only way you can deal with one of these rare phenomena **is to smash through it and take the hits**.

This is because avoiding them and taking the path of least resistance will take your ship off course, quite probably towards a black hole. This will inevitably cause a mission failure and send you back the way you came.

Know that good days always follow bad days.

Quitting in the moment on a bad day is easy. Turning your ship around on a bad day is easy: some recruits have even quit when they were right on course for their breakthrough to make it to Starship Commander, but they didn't believe it.

Your ability to deal with asteroids and aliens will be down to your resilience and persistence as a human being. It will depend on the daily habits you have exercised, leading right up to this point. How do the chemicals in your body react to situations you see as threatening? Do you fight, do you flee, do you freeze?

Mostly, your response will now be down to some of the lessons you learned in T -8 Sickbay. You need to ask yourself a series of questions. How much do you value your place on this mission? What is your reason for being here? Do you have a strong enough WHY power? And what are the consequences of turning your ship around and heading back to earth? What's back home for you? Something's missing back there, otherwise you wouldn't be here in the first place –

– and you wouldn't have this book in your hands. The thing is, if you decide to return home, that same thing will be missing. There's nothing back there for you other than what you had before.

Do your goals and plans supersede your work and interests?

Do you know where you're going, what you want and how to get there? Or are you merely existing day to day? That is, living out the same routine and indulging in the same habits that satisfy a temporary need for relief but ultimately keep you going round in circles and holding you back from any kind of progression towards the life you've always dreamed about? Your ability to keep your ship on the correct trajectory, even when faced with these obstacles, will depend on whether you're in pursuit of a higher goal or purpose with a carefully thought out and mapped out plan. Or ... is your autopilot simply repeating the same day over and over again?

An asteroid hurtling toward you and an alien attacking you or gravity pulling you back is a reminder that you're heading for greater things!

T -2

YOUR STORY

Phew, you survived ...

... but don't relax just yet. We want you to spend some time to reflect on the journey so far. Think about and recall everything you've encountered in this short space of time: the people you've spoken to and maybe helped, and the experiences you've had and shared with those on the same journey. The aliens and asteroids you've encountered and how you overcame them, and what damage you may have taken to your ship. What has been the most important learning curve for you so far?

Have you noted any of these things at the back of this book for review? And is your priority list at the back of this handbook looking good?

We've saved one of the most important lessons for the end: a lesson you must fully understand before you can become a Starship Commander. We thought we'd wait until your ship broke out of the atmosphere before we spoke about **your social currency.** Now that you're experiencing weightlessness you can unbuckle, float about, spin around and look back at the planet you've just left. You can't buy your way to this point. Your ticket purchase got you on board this ship – but it's your hard work and persistence so far that have got you bursting up through the clouds. You should be proud of how far you've come. I know *we* are!

This lesson is all about understanding that the only currency you have to spend up here in space **is your stories.** You may ask, what on earth does that mean?

YOUR SOCIAL CURRENCY IS YOUR STORY

Your money got you on board this ship ... but that's it. After that, money is meaningless in respect of your success on this mission. What's far more valuable than the money you've invested are the stories you will collect, and may have already collected as a result of your work getting this ship off the ground.

Money can't buy you stories – it's only hard work that generates them.

Money gets spent, but stories can be used over and over again until the day you die. Those same stories will be used to attract future people to your journey and ultimately give you the life you've dreamed of. Your focus of personal financial reward needs to be changed to helping others find their reward. Doing this will build up so much future currency that your journey will be fuelled for years.

YOUR CHILDHOOD

When you were a child the stories you were told and the stories you made up formed the backbone of your very existence. Didn't you ever dream of going into space or flying on a ship or maybe meeting alien life forms? Just because you are grown up now, don't think for one minute that stories have lost their power!

Your parents probably taught you not to speak to strangers and not to tell stories (by which they meant inventing them). While this advice may have served you in youth, like so many of the lessons we were taught by the adults around us they don't benefit us in adulthood. For example, safety is a lesson that protects us as children. But you're not a child any more! Your desire and need to be safe and comfortable on this mission will always be a trade-off against the ability to achieve what you want. No journey to the stars is a safe journey, and that's why you'll collect some great stories along the way.

UNTIL NOW

Nobody has been very interested in your story ...well, not really. On earth, we exist in a place where so many people just don't listen – even worse, they don't care! Most humans are more concerned with talking about themselves and promoting their own fantastic achievements, blissfully unaware of other people's needs or desires to be heard. It is for this reason that so many people are struggling in life – yet they can't work out why.

You can't give your ego full rein and improve yourself at the same time any more than you can be sure you're fine and get better at the same time. You will have to deal with many paradoxical ideas like this on your trip. Listening was always an instruction in school. It was a 'do or be punished' kind of idea. **So most people are tired of listening**. They want a voice, they want a platform.

Now you come along and you can be different. **You can create success through listening to people and solving other people's problems**. Give them a platform to be heard; you can be the platform. You can make people fall in love with you just by listening to them – but your natural inclination will always be to solve your own problems first. This is another paradoxical idea that can hold you back from all you dream of.

Sharing your stories and talking about yourself are two completely different things

If you're going to share your story with people, the first thing that you need to understand is that you must position yourself to be able to do this. That is, do people want to hear it? Why should people give *you* a platform to be heard? People will only be interested in your story when you have connected and formed a relationship, built trust and **shown in a sincere way that you care about them**. This can all happen in five minutes if you work at it. But if you don't invest time in getting to know people, **they just hear you, but they don't care**. If you can master the most basic of human skill of listening, then the power of sharing your own story and being heard will become much greater. **The real truth is that people aren't interested in your journey**. They're interested in **how your journey can help them**. That is what they're looking for – they're looking for hope.

PEOPLE WANT YOUR HELP WITHOUT YOU SELLING IT TO THEM

This is where the power of stories comes in. **That's your social currency**. Most people are looking for something that can break the monotony of their existence and something that can instil some progression in their life. They know, deep down in the bottom of their soul, that they need this journey too. In the end, though, that will only happen **through the stories you share** and **not by you telling** them they need it.

We highlighted in T -2 that your past and present achievements are important to a degree – but there needs to be **nobility to your story**, or it will be harder for people to connect with you. They need to be **attracted enough to want to listen to you**. People want to hear about your struggle, not your glory. They want to hear about who you've

86

helped, not how you've helped yourself. They want to hear about where you've come from, not where you're going. If you're reaching for the stars, if you're heading for the moon and beyond, nobody is likely to be interested in that. They want to know why you're going there, what happened on earth and in your life to help you shape that choice. Having the pot of gold at the end of the rainbow is not the key! **It's why the gold is important to you**. What does this mission mean? And how will it impact the lives of others you're close to?

Attracting people to you on this mission will be key to its longevity and the size of your success. Be aware that it relies on your ability to keep **continually growing your list** of contacts as opposed to **depleting and burning out your list** to a point where you're convinced there's nobody left to speak to on the entire planet. The only way to grow your list and to have people to speak to for years to come is to continue to share stories and so continue to attract people to you.

Remember, part of your mission is to help change people's emotional state for the better. If you can do this, they'll continue to talk about you in a positive way for ever. The more people you help, the more stories you will have to share. Even when asteroids hit you or aliens attack, there's still a story to share because it's not the end of the story that matters – it's the meaning behind it.

People want to hear about your struggle and how you overcame adversity. So asteroids and aliens can be used to your advantage …

You may be able to inspire people in a few moments with the great things that you've done – **but they'll forget about you almost**

immediately. If you want to be remembered and spoken about in a positive way, then you will need to continue to bring value to people's lives by **helping them out of their pain**.

Your greatest accomplishments won't be the changes you've created for yourself but the changes you've created for so many other people around you. Recruits who focus too much on a pot of gold are the first to be disappointed. The stories you collect will provide the futureproofing you need for your journey. The stories you acquire over the next 90 days will be told in years to come.

You've made it this far, so you already have a story, maybe a collection of stories. That will attract more people to you than you can ever imagine. You don't get to relive your first 90 days. You can always launch over and over again – but you never get back your first 90 days! If that time has passed, then start again from now and make sure your new recruits get this message. Through the process of invitation, as covered in T -5, and speaking to people you know and meet, you'll collect a story for each one.

Every positive and negative response can be used in a story that can be shared over and over again. This is what the people of earth want to see and hear.

What's your story so far?

T-1

THE SCIENCE OF FICTION

Decades ago, the thought of venturing into space was ridiculous. Even flying was a notion that most believed would not be possible, never mind putting a human on the moon. But now, in the early 21st century, the idea that civilian passengers will soon be able to take a trip into space is firmly on the radar. Now here you are with a chance to do what most will never do. What many still believe isn't possible. Not because it isn't, though, but because that's what their environment has taught them.

Belief in something is a state of mind in which a person thinks something to be the case without the empirical evidence to prove it. That's incredibly valuable: every individual who's ever accomplished anything new has one thing in common: vision and an utter belief in what they're doing, way before they can see any evidence that it would work.

Look at how far you've come since the beginning of the trip. Right now, you may feel like you're not where you need or want to be in life. You may feel as though your ship's still parked on the launch pad. You may be telling yourself the story that there is no evidence to suggest that this mission will be or can be a success, or that it's even achievable by you. You must be wary of that voice in your head. Because what we can tell you is that if you've made it this far, your ship has well and truly left the atmosphere.

As you're reading this right now, you may be looking back at the earth and working alongside your Starship Commander or somebody who's mentoring and guiding you. Other people who have led successful missions and gone on to help others are doing the same. Why not you? Our final request to you is to ask you to take their belief on board if you can't summon your own. Your Starship Commander won't take you to a place they've not been to themselves. Trust in the process; you have absolutely nothing to lose and everything to gain.

As this point, as we approach the end of the first of many missions, you still have your whole future and millions of miles ahead of you.

The road to failure is paved with people who believe that their past determined their future, because the past is the only reality we know. But your current situation is not the end. What you have right now is not all you'll ever have. Do you remember what we said about reality at the beginning of this book? **Your reality is most likely inaccurate**.

Your programming over the last few decades has taught you to focus on:

Your work and your interests, not your goals and plans.

These are not mutually exclusive. You don't have to **give up your need to work and have fun** but you do need to **give priority to your goals and your plans**, and how you're going to achieve them. **This doesn't mean giving something up;** it simply means a shift of focus, switching priorities to make room for something of a higher order. You must re-address the balance, starting now! Your focus needs to shift away from what gives you instant relief and satisfaction right now, to work on the things that aren't immediately visible, like your ship passing Mars a few months from now.

Believing in **what will be** is much harder than **believing in what is or what has been**. Where you are right now in your life is not the end of the journey. Your journey is not yet written, but unless you have a clear picture in your mind of where your journey's headed it will be written for you by somebody else – and then it's very unlikely to arrive at the ending you want! This isn't a sci-fi movie; the good guys don't always win in the end.

Belief in an idea is hard, but **as soon as you start to work on the plan, things become easier** and you become happier. If you feel that your ship is still placed in an upright position on that launch pad, the hardest thing to do is step inside and fire up the controls. But as soon as you have lift off, that sense of progression will kick in. That's the feeling that you're searching for, that's what you want! Your ship is far more dangerous to you when kept on the launch pad than it is shooting through the sky. This is because it's not doing what it's been designed to do, which is to head for the stars. Human beings are the same; we're not designed to stay still. Look around you at the things you see on earth right now. Is there any evidence to suggest that everybody's happy and content, and heading in the direction they want? That's because upward is the only place you can find happiness, but just about everybody is looking down!

Most human beings are not doing what they were built to do. They are doing what they've been programmed from birth to do; for 97 per cent of humans on earth, their ships are still waiting to launch. Their environment has taught them that it's better, safer, to keep it on the ground. When the actions you perform don't marry with what your heart and mind are telling you, the chemicals in your brain make you unhappy. This is not a good state of mind for space flight.

What you have or don't have isn't the cause of your feelings. **The cause is what you're *not* doing about what you want** – that's the problem.

Every Starship Commander that came before you knew this. Trust in the mission and what you've learned, and the journey will take care of itself.

TO BE CONTINUED ...

FOR MORE INFORMATION

Please visit:

www.mindsetbeforematter.com

or...

Facebook: **David J Ross**

For more great trainings, tips and 6- and 7-figure earner interviews – join David on **Facebook live, Mondays @ 8.30pm**

Mindset Before Matter' – 'For Your Network Marketing Journey' is now available in **Print, Kindle** and **Audio** from **www.mindsetbeforematter.com**

RECOMMENDED READING

Beach Money, by Jordan Adler

Building Your Network Marketing Business, by Jim Rohn

Fearless Networking, by Todd Falcone

Go for No! by Andrea Waltz and Richard Fenton

Go for No! for Network Marketing, by Andrea Waltz, Richard Fenton and Ray Higdon

Go Pro: 7 Steps to Becoming a Network Marketing Professional, by Eric Worre

How Full is your Bucket? by Tom Rath and Donald O Clifton

How to Win Friends and Influence People, by Dale Carnegie

The Compound Effect, by Darren Hardy

The Four Year Career, by Richard Brooke

The Game of Networking, Rob Sperry

The Magic of Thinking Big, by David J Schwartz

The Miracle Morning for Network Marketers, by Hal Elrod , Pat Petrini & Honoree Corder

The Slight Edge, by Jeff Olson

Think & Grow Rich, by Napoleon Hill

What to Say When You Talk to Yourself, by Shad Helmstetter

The Prospecting Game, by Wes Linden

The Impact System, by Stephan Longworth

YOUR PRIORITY BOARDING LIST

WHAT YOU NEED TO DO NEXT

YOUR CONTACTS LIST

YOUR FIRST 30

Mindset Before Matter

MISSION NOTES

Lightning Source UK Ltd.
Milton Keynes UK
UKHW02f0945160118
316239UK00001B/44/P